AGENCY
RECRUITMENT 101

The Ultimate Insider's Guide
to this Business and Career

DANDAN ZHU

Copyright © 2023 Dandan Zhu

All rights reserved. No part of this book may be reproduced in any form or used in any manner without the prior written permission of the copyright owner, publisher, or author, except as permitted by U.S. copyright law.

This publication is designed to provide accurate and authoritative information in regard to the subject matter covered. It is sold with the understanding that neither the author nor the publisher is engaged in rendering legal, investment, accounting, or other professional services. While the publisher and author have used their best efforts in preparing this book, they make no representations or warranties with respect to the accuracy or completeness of the contents of this book and specifically disclaim any implied warranties of merchantability or fitness for a particular purpose. No warranty may be created or extended by sales representatives or written sales materials. The advice and strategies contained herein may not be suitable for your situation. You should consult with a professional when appropriate. Neither the publisher nor the author shall be liable for any loss of profit or any other commercial damages, including but not limited to special, incidental, consequential, personal, or other damages.

To request permissions, contact the publisher at dz@dandanzhu.com

Paperback: 979-8-89109-319-5

Ebook: 979-8-89109-320-1

First edition 2023

Dandan Zhu

New York, NY

dandanzhu.com

www.agencyrecruitment101.com

TABLE OF CONTENTS

Letter from Dandan 1

Intro: Welcome to AR101 5

Chapter 1: My Agency Recruitment Journey 15

Chapter 2: What is Agency Recruitment Exactly? 25

Chapter 3: The Agency Recruitment Market 37

Chapter 4: The Agency Recruitment Process 49

Chapter 5: Direct Hire Recruitment 65

Chapter 6: Staffing 85

Chapter 7: Compensation Components 103

Chapter 8: Commission 111

Chapter 9: The Agency Recruitment Career Ladder 131

Chapter 10: Traits of Top Billers 143

Chapter 11: Recruitment Tools 155

Chapter 12: Launch Your Career! 165

Chapter 13: Next Steps and Tips for Success 171

LETTER FROM DANDAN

Hi Go-Getters,

Welcome to the fascinating world of agency recruitment!

I am beyond excited that you've decided to explore this potentially life-changing profession.

Get ready to unlock a treasure trove of insider insights in *Agency Recruitment 101* (AR101), your ultimate guide to this business and career.

By the end of AR101, you'll have all the knowledge you need to make a confident decision about your path ahead!

As you dive into the book, it's important to know this brutal truth:

Very few people make it in agency recruitment.

The reason why is two-fold:

Firstly, it's a tough and competitive sales job that many people find difficult.

Secondly, many people who start their career in this business don't know what they're getting themselves into, so their expectations aren't aligned with the demands of the daily grind, resulting in burnout.

In other words, if people were more *informed* about the reality of agency recruitment and *intentional* with this career, it would lead to more success, lower exit rates, and improvement of how recruiters are perceived by the general public as a result.

This is why I wrote AR101!

Having started in this sales profession at age 23, I adopted the mindset to continuously improve and become the best at what I do.

Fast forward 5 years: at the age of 28, I achieved FIRE (Financial Independence, Retire Early) by investing the high commissions I earned through recruitment into cash-flowing real estate assets which continued to grow, making me a millionaire by 30.

Without this ability to control and increase my income exponentially by leveraging agency recruitment at such a young age, there would be few, *if any*, opportunities I qualified for that could build me anywhere close to that level of wealth!

My personal experience coupled with seeing many other agency recruiters achieve the same thing, has caused me to become a rabid advocate and evangelist for this business and career.

It is undoubtedly a viable profession *any* ambitious person can find financial success and freedom within.

My dream and goal is to shout from the rooftops how recruitment changed my life so more people can understand and access this career opportunity to help them get ahead!

The more amazing, talented people who know about this industry, the better the quality of new entrants who launch their careers in our line of work. In turn, this will cause our *entire* profession to benefit because the overall commitment and competency level of agency recruiters will rise.

To support this mission, my recruitment business, DG Recruit (Est. 2018), coaches, trains, and partners with aspiring and existing agency recruiters to launch and progress their agency careers.

In line with the concept of The Venn Diagram of Purpose, created by Andrés Zuzunaga, a Spanish astrologer and entrepreneur, this personal goal fulfills all four elements of what brings me joy and happiness personally and professionally.

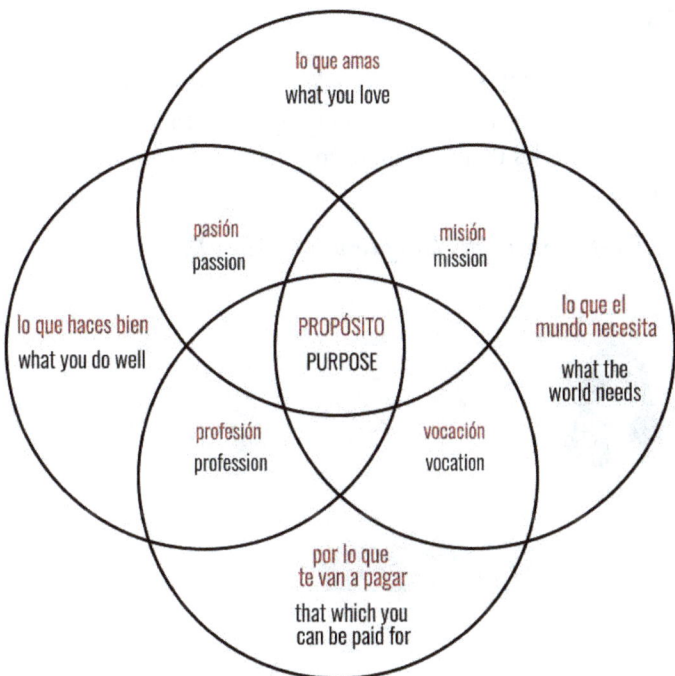

Agency recruitment allows me to do something I enjoy doing (calling and engaging with people is fun!), what the world desperately needs (specialists to solve labor gap problems and support passive talent), that pays well (placement fees are lucrative), and what I can do well (as a top biller, I'm highly efficient at placing people into new roles).

It's a privilege to share this intel with like-minded individuals who want to find an enjoyable profession that can lead to financial freedom without requiring expensive graduate degrees.

With my experience working within this profession and now recruiting for it, I've distilled all the key information you need to know into AR101. This is *the* ultimate insider's guide to arm you with comprehensive knowledge even pros may not know!

For more recruitment training, coaching, and webinar events with me, join the AR101 Facebook group at facebook.com/groups/agencyrecruitment101 and sign-up to dandanzhu.com so we can keep in touch.

After reading AR101, if you're ready to launch your recruitment career, take our course, recruiterprep.com, to access 3 action-packed modules that will guide you through the entire job search process.

Without further ado, let's jump into AR101!

INTRO: WELCOME TO AR101

What this book is all about

AR101 is the ultimate insider's guide to the business and career of agency recruitment. This niche sales profession empowers ambitious go-getters to achieve financial success while developing skills bound to be useful in all facets of life and work!

As one of the many agency recruiters who leveraged this career to become a millionaire by 30, I wish more people knew about this profession.

It changed my life; it could change *yours*, too.

Unfortunately, due to how obscure this career remains, the majority of people don't even know about this career!

Through my work recruiting for agency recruiters, I've spoken to thousands of agency recruiters throughout the years. Most randomly fall into this career while others get referred in by their friends. Either way, it's rare to hear about agency recruiters intentionally making their way into the career path.

Due to the widespread lack of awareness of what's possible in this business and career, the agency recruitment industry *itself* faces a labor shortage!

Worse yet, many who enter this line of work find it *by accident*. Because so many people try out this career without any knowledge beforehand, they end up quickly finding out later that they do not enjoy it, don't do well at it, and as a result, only have negative things to say about it!

They then perpetuate negativity about this career path when the opposite is true for many of us who have leveraged this opportunity to build incredible lifestyles for ourselves and our families.

To combat the misinformation from naysaying people who failed in their agency recruitment careers, I wrote AR101 to set the record straight!

I am passionate about spreading more information about this career, so more people can discover this lucrative, exciting, and fun profession.

This career has the potential to be life changing and my genuine wish is that more people will use this book as a resource to make an *informed* decision if they should pursue this career option or not.

As an industry insider, I will give you the good, the bad, and the ugly so that you can make the right judgment call without wasting your time finding out the hard way.

If the information shared in AR101 resonates with you, then great! AR101 will equip you with expert knowledge and tips to launch your career and set yourself up to crush it right out of the gate!

A word of caution though…

Making the big bucks is rarely a simple endeavor. Most millionaires aren't created by 20 hour workweeks.

This is a tried and true sales career you can leverage to build wealth as many have done time and time again, *however you have to be willing to put in the work.*

It *will* be hard work, make no mistake about it!

Agency recruitment is a sales job, so regardless of economic cycle, experience level, and macro market forces, people who put in the work consistently will survive and thrive.

Time and time again, savvy and hardworking go-getters leverage this business and career to create an incredible lifestyle, but it comes at a cost. The work is never easy, smooth sailing, or overnight.

As with most high income jobs, exceptional people who work exceptionally hard end up earning the lion's share.

Furthermore, the earlier you get started in this industry, the larger your advantage is. Many agency recruiters start their careers within 1-5 years of graduating college.

Because success compounds quickly over time and so many get their start at such an early life stage, this business has the capacity to churn out young millionaires, year in and year out.

Here are some *real* success stories from the industry:

A salesperson with 2 years of experience from another field started his career at a national recruitment agency. He became a top rookie then top biller. His income grew from $160k to $300k over the years. 5 years in, he broke off to start his own recruitment firm. In his first year of working as a solo recruitment producer, he earned over $900k for himself. He's not even 33 years old!

A former SaaS sales specialist at age 26 didn't like the industry and product she was selling and by chance, stumbled into one of my Quora articles about how recruitment changed my life so she got in touch. From there, my recruitment firm, DG Recruit, worked to place her at one of our recruitment firm clients specializing in energy recruitment where she became a global top biller, earning more than 6-figures every single year. After learning the business at her first firm, she has now moved on to a boutique recruitment firm where she is a senior leader.

An ex-dancer on top TV talent shows pivoted into recruitment after a dance career-ending injury in his late 20s. He worked hard, performed well, and finally achieved his dream of breaking over 6-figures in recruitment income in his first year as a top biller. Due to the low pay in the arts field, he was previously never able to pay off debt and build his net worth. Through his new career in agency recruitment, he is debt free, can now afford to buy real estate, and ready to really start stacking up his net worth by buying equities and other assets, something he could never have achieved through his previous job.

A law school graduate after a few years of practicing at big corporate law firms decided he didn't want to continue his journey in law, instead discovering recruitment in his late 20s. Due to his natural sales and people skills, he became a top biller right away, making over $250k-$300k for the 2 years at the legal recruitment firm he worked at. Then he broke off to start his own recruitment firm, personally doubling his income in his first year of business, now thriving as a solopreneur running his own practice.

This isn't abnormal or shocking. My personal experience and the stories that I have from top billers who left uninspiring jobs and situations to find their success in recruitment are plentiful.

To access more success stories and real-life examples, check out my YouTube page (youtube.com/dandanzhudg) and the DG Recruit Podcast (dandanzhu.com/podcasts) which features interviews with top billers from all over the world.

If more people knew that recruitment can be as financially and professionally rewarding as other career tracks highly touted by society, the general public, and the media, then our industry would have truly "made it" as a mainstream career choice, which is not the case presently.

There is no doubt that this profession has the potential to change lives; many case studies prove this reality. Before jumping on the bandwagon though, read this next segment carefully.

What you NEED to know about this Career

In order to ensure that you'll get the most out of AR101, please review these 7 disclaimers about the agency recruitment career before you dive into the rest of the book:

1. **This book is about *agency recruitment*, NOT to be confused with Human Resources (HR) related fields.**

Agency recruitment is commonly mislabeled and lumped incorrectly with other fields, namely HR, internal/corporate recruiting, talent acquisition (TA), organizational behavior, human capital, etc.

Agency recruitment is a career *in and of itself*. It is a type of niche *sales* job, not to be confused with an internal support function like HR and TA.

AR101 would be the wrong book to read if you're looking to pursue a career in the human capital field, HR space, or internal recruitment/TA specialisms.

AR101 only focuses on what it's like to work at recruitment and staffing *agencies* which are sales organizations that specifically provide this niche professional service.

2. Agency recruitment is a sales job, not a technical role.

Agency recruitment is a sales job that fulfills the sole function of generating revenue and high commission opportunity, usually paid out on top of a low salary and limited benefits.

If you're more comfortable with a traditional "stable" corporate career path that is compensated primarily by a high guaranteed salary, then this would not be the right career for you.

Not only is commission compensation never guaranteed, you'd have to possess incredibly thick skin to handle the stigma, challenge of securing and handling customer demands, and tough workload of being in a sales role.

Thus, this sales career requires quite a bit of fortitude and relentlessness to drive a high volume of customer contact to win market share. As a result, the income top agency recruiters are paid outpaces many other career tracks.

3. Recruitment is a hard job that takes consistency, time, and a sustained investment of effort to succeed at.

Recruitment is not a "get rich quick (and easy)" scheme.

Don't get me wrong; you can get rich relatively quickly in this role since some first and second year recruiters earn over $100k-$200k yearly. However, that's not guaranteed to be the case for everyone!

Most people will not achieve this level of earning overnight. A big part of it depends on the agency you start working at, how hard you work, your natural affinity for the role, and how well you're set up to succeed personally and professionally.

Success will take significant effort; luck alone is not enough to win.

The brutal truth is that to become a millionaire, like this career can help you achieve, you have to work hard at it, *consistently*.

There is little room for making excuses, victim mentality, or an "anything goes, get to it when I get to it" approach.

Agency recruitment IS hustle culture - without urgency, hard work, and dedication, it is hard to survive and thrive due to the competitive nature of the business and commercial landscape.

4. **Recruitment is a cutthroat business, contrary to popular belief.**

I will be blunt when speaking about how brutal this industry and career track is; agency recruitment is a serious business, not a hobby, fun gig, or altruistic pursuit.

Transparently, agency recruitment is not particularly forgiving in terms of providing people an unlimited amount of time to prove themselves.

In recruitment, there is little value placed on participation trophies and feel good fluff. Results are the only thing that matters.

Being that the purpose of this book is to help you seriously understand this profession, *honesty* is key. I do not mean to offend, hurt, or disempower anyone. Instead of only selling you on the good and glamorous stuff, in AR101, I'll be fair in sharing insights from all angles.

5. **Recruitment is not a cushy gig - it is a full-time grind.**

When people hear about the lucrative placement fees agency recruiters get, their attention is rightfully peaked. However, many people go wrong by underestimating how much work goes into building a successful recruitment practice.

Many people start a recruitment practice without ever having worked a day at a proper recruitment firm before. They don't know what they don't know and lack proper training. Even worse, some people assume recruitment is something they can side-hustle when it's actually a full-time grind!

The agency recruitment lifestyle is the *polar opposite* of a cushy corporate job; you have to earn your success in this business.

In many similarly high paying professions, at the outset you cannot expect work-life balance, 6-figure base salaries, the red carpet treatment, or 32-hour work weeks.

Perhaps this is one of the *key* reasons many people quit the biz. They want more of what I call the "perk-life", prioritizing benefits instead of commission reward.

Top producers, however, understand the inverse relationship between perceived comfort and actual reward. While many other jobs may seem more glamorous and comfortable, the actual financial opportunity to increase overall income potential in those salary-heavy professions is low and slow growing.

Thus, they'd rather sacrifice in the short term, work hard, and reap the rewards of their success leveraging this sales career's incredible commission opportunity.

If this resonates with you, your prospects in this career path are certainly promising.

6. **Recruitment is track, *not* soccer.**

Agency recruitment is more of a single-player sport because commission plans at most agencies are largely set up to incentivize and reward individuals, not teams.

Like many other sales careers, personal achievement is prized and monitored in agency recruitment as well. While every recruiter likely works within a specific division or team, they're responsible to hit their *own* billing targets.

Oftentimes and eventually, you'll have to compete against your colleagues in order to get ahead at work, fighting for the right to work with certain clients and candidates.

Furthermore, not only will you have to compete internally, you'll face external competition from outside competitors that you have to grab market share from and sell against to win clients over.

Those who need more handholding or rely on help from others to stay on task will struggle in this career because most top performers are self-reliant and prioritize their own success in this performance-based profession.

At the end of the day, *personal* success is the name of the game so agency recruitment rewards those with high levels of *personal* accountability, independence, self-motivation, and self discipline.

7. **The earlier in your professional career that you join agency recruitment, the higher your odds of succeeding.**

The vast majority of agency recruiters start this career within 1-7 years of finishing an undergrad degree, myself included.

There are many reasons for this phenomenon, but the long and short of it is this:

People at later stages of their careers may not accept the low base salaries offered in agency recruitment.

Most people can't afford to take a low base, high commission role at a time in their life where fixed costs are rising and personal situations demand higher guaranteed income.

Due to this financial constraint, people in earlier stages of life are more likely to accept a low base structure, which is why the majority of agencies that hire and train large classes of entry level recruiters recruit graduates directly from universities or focus on early career professionals with some sales experience.

Furthermore, the immense stress, all-encompassing time commitment, and stamina required to succeed in this role would be unrealistic and harder to take on at a later time where there are competing priorities.

AR101 will continue sharing more considerations worth mulling over so that you can evaluate the impact this profession may have on your life.

If these 7 disclaimers do not deter you, then agency recruitment may be the right profession and business for you yet!

What AR101 will teach you

If you're ready to dive into this lucrative and unique sales career, AR101 is the perfect resource to help you understand this profession deeply.

After sharing my agency recruitment career journey in Chapter 1, we'll jump right into terminology, definitions, and what this business is all about in Chapter 2.

You'll learn more about the recruitment market and industry as a whole in Chapter 3, followed by a step-by-step rundown of the entire recruitment process in Chapter 4.

Chapter 5 and Chapter 6 goes over the two types of recruitment, direct hire and staffing, respectively, showing you how recruitment firms partner with companies to solve a variety of hiring needs.

Chapter 7 is where we talk about the good stuff - compensation! You'll get the insider's scoop on the wide range of financial incentives and rewards available to agency recruiters.

Chapter 8 further delves into the complicated topic of recruitment commission, an esoteric subject fully broken down so you can see the broad range of plans available.

Just like all professions, recruitment has its own career ladder, detailed in Chapter 9 followed by Chapter 10 which goes over the top traits successful agency recruiters commonly exhibit.

Recruitment has come a long way with a number of technology tools and resources proliferating which Chapter 11 discusses, including commentary on AI products.

If you're ready to jump into the recruitment game, Chapter 12 walks through the most common ways to get your start into the industry, along with final tips and next steps to consider in Chapter 13 as you embark on your journey to pursue this career.

By the end of AR101, you'll have mastered all the details about this exciting profession to a level that many people already doing the job may not even know!

Most importantly, you may discover a newfound understanding and hopefully, appreciation of what agency recruitment professionals do.

Without further ado, let's get started!

Chapter Highlights:

- AR101 is your comprehensive resource chock full of insider insights on every aspect of this business and career.
- Agency recruitment is a sales job, not a technical or support role.
- Please read through the 7 disclaimers carefully to ensure that you're aligned with and fully understanding of the demands of this profession to reach success.
- You can achieve financial success relatively quickly in this role, but it will take consistency, time, and a sustained investment of effort.
- Recruitment is not a hobby, a side hustle, or an experiment; it is a serious business, profession, and industry.
- In recruitment, personal success is the name of the game due to its competitive nature.

Recommended Resources:

- If you want to learn more about agency recruitment on the go, make sure to check out the DG Recruit Podcast (dandanzhu.com/podcasts/dgrecruitpodcast) which includes training, information, and interviews with top agency recruitment professionals so you can hear about their career journeys, key learnings, and experiences.
- If you're ready to get started, take the Recruiter Prep (recruiterprep.com) course now to launch your career in 3 straightforward modules.

CHAPTER 1

MY AGENCY RECRUITMENT JOURNEY

Started from the Bottom...

In 2009, I graduated with a Bachelor's degree in Finance, right when the financial world imploded in the worst recession since the Great Depression.

Fate couldn't have been more cruel as all the finance jobs disappeared overnight. Thankfully, my family's small business, a Chinese restaurant in Boston, was in dire need of help, so at least I could be of use to run their restaurant while figuring out "what now?".

With student and car debt looming over me, I had no time to despair.

When my day was over at the restaurant, I hustled hard to apply to hundreds of jobs in desperate hopes of finding some formal career path to embark on.

By sheer luck, I came across an obscure career that completely changed my life in ways I could never have imagined.

Enter Agency Recruitment

By a fluke, a recruitment firm saw my application for a financial analyst role.

Their internal recruiter called me, not for the finance position that I applied to, but to persuade me of something I had no idea about:

Was I open to considering the field of agency recruitment by joining their recruitment firm instead?

In other words, would I be interested to become a headhunter for this recruiting agency?

Since I didn't know a thing about agency recruitment, I was intrigued to at least learn more.

They pitched it to me as a *sales* job, not to be confused with the typical Human Resources (HR)/internal recruiter support function I thought "recruitment" meant.

Quite the contrary: *Agency* recruiters, aka recruiters or headhunters who work at recruitment agencies, sell candidates to clients and jobs to candidates. They're professional *salespeople*.

Every time a successful match is made, lucrative commissions are paid out. The more placements a recruiter makes, the more money they take home due to the power of commission income.

The Journey Begins

Since I wanted a high-paying career straight out of that gate, I was immediately drawn to the meritocratic nature of this niche sales job.

Unlike traditional salary-heavy jobs that require you to climb a career ladder, recruitment would immediately reward you financially if you're better than your peers.

Inherently, that appealed to me because I disliked my past internships where everyone was paid the same wage regardless of performance. Even if you were *twice* as good as someone else, your paycheck would only reflect a *marginal* difference due to most jobs lacking the power to pay out on a performance basis.

Thus, in January 2011, I took the leap of faith to move to New York City to try my hand at agency recruitment on a $35k base to seek my fortune.

I figured, what was there to lose?

Walking onto the busy sales floor, I knew I made the right call. Immediately, I felt a sizzle of excitement that I never experienced before in any of my relatively boring internships doing analyst and admin-type activities.

Energy crackled through the air as top billers landed big placement fees. Young people sauntered around like hotshots with Rolexes on their wrists and 6-figure incomes. People were laughing and joking with each other and yapping up a storm with their customers on the phone. These people were doing something I wanted to be a part of.

Upon seeing what was possible, I immediately yearned for their level of success and career fulfillment.

Unlike my previously lackluster efforts in my boring internships (and school in general) which I considered pure drudgery and misery, I knew that recruitment was something entirely different.

Instead of dreading this "adult" job, my first *real* job, I actually looked forward to it because I knew it would get me to where I wanted to be: rich and successful *ASAP*.

Sales Career of Millionaires

What I didn't know then was that the top agency recruitment professionals are literally worth millions of dollars!

After learning the craft, they quickly can produce close to or over 7 figures of revenue for their firms due to the fee structure in high value recruitment markets.

By enriching their firms through closing deals, the financial gains earn agency recruitment professionals multiple 6-figures (millions over time) in the form of commissions *per* year!

Through this sales career, multiple people found their pathway to wealth with many becoming certified millionaires in their late 20s and early 30s.

This profession not only had the potential of making me rich but it was something that I could envision enjoying on a daily basis. What could be better than being paid a lot of money while doing something you enjoy? That is literally a dream come true!

If they could do it, *why not me?*

I had the audacity to dream that I *could*. Because goddamnit, I wanted to be successful, to amount to something, to break free from the limitations of financial dearth, toiling everyday for another dollar just to survive.

As they say, get rich or die trying, right? Time to carpe diem; I vowed to make the most of it.

How Agency Recruitment Changed Everything

With this vision of glory in mind, I got to work as an agency recruiter. And it *was* hard work!

I stayed late. I worked weekends. I learned from other top billers. I did exactly what I was told and more. I worked like my future depended on it—because it did!

Within my first year in recruiting in 2011, I became a global top rookie, earning $87k, well above what I thought was possible.

In year 2, I achieved top biller status again, almost doubling my first year billings, earning over $130k.

By year 3, I was clocking in over $215k as a 25 year old, dominating my market and solidifying my standing as a record-setter, confident in my skillset as an agency recruitment professional.

That year, my biggest *monthly* commission check topped over $60k and my yearly income tax bill alone was over $90k (thank you, NYC tax rates!).

To see that my tax bill alone was more than what most people earn in a year (certainly more than what I earned year 1!) really put things in perspective of how far agency recruitment can take you if you stick with it.

Don't Just Earn, SAVE!

As my income grew rapidly through my recruitment job, I got ahead in the wealth-building game by adhering to the Wealth Trifecta Strategy I created.

The first step is earning as much as you can. In sales jobs like agency recruitment, I had already achieved that by becoming a top biller and high earner.

The second step of the Wealth Trifecta Strategy is saving.

Instead of upgrading my lifestyle the more money I made (lifestyle inflation), I maintained relatively similar financial habits centered around frugality, delayed gratification, and self restraint when it came to spending.

Anything to save money was a smart move worthy of celebration and stubborn adherence. I'd go to shameless lengths to save and reduce costs. No discount was beneath my pride to ask for.

I'd commonly choose to inconvenience myself to save money, once flying 29 hours each way for cheaper airfare, never opted for taxis even late at night, and regularly ate cheap foods like hotdogs, dollar menu items at McDonald's, discounted sushi, and Subway's $5 foot-longs.

Most importantly, I renthacked, saving the biggest robber of personal wealth - rent. Instead of renting a nice apartment by myself, I acquired leases as a sublandlord and rented out the available rooms, decreasing my portion of the rent to a few hundred bucks a month, an unbelievable cost savings.

Through it all, I prioritized my career in agency recruitment as I built up multiple markets for my employer including the executive search division, helping venture capital funds and top biotech businesses find C-level executives to earn even bigger fees ($90k-$100k was a regular deal size I was handling at that point, pretty insane).

Don't just Save, INVEST!

The third and last leg of the Wealth Trifecta is investing. As the money came in from recruiting, I feverishly started studying real estate investing.

Having seen plenty of people haul in some major wins in real estate, I was decently aware how powerfully life changing the gains from real estate can be. Plus, I was already familiar with that whole grind having helped my mother many summers and weekends on DIY projects for her rental properties when I was a teen.

With the people skills I learned through recruiting and the tenant management experience I gained through renthacking, I felt confident that landlording would be the perfect next challenge.

On weekends, and during/after work, I started obsessively stalking the market on various real estate apps to find prime locations and investment opportunities.

Since my recruitment income was so high, banks could safely lend to me. Because of my extreme savings and investment strategies, I also had the 20% down payment ready to go to successfully close on my first two investment properties I bought in short succession.

Time to Go Solo

By age 28, due to how quickly my real estate holdings appreciated, I accumulated enough personal wealth to eliminate the need for employment. In essence, I reached FIRE (Financial Independence, Retire Early).

With my youth, skills, lack of dependents, good health, and financial cushion that my real estate assets provided, it was the perfect time to quit corporate America, once and for all.

Without a backward glance, I quit my $200k+ job a week after my 5th year anniversary at the firm, barrelling straight into entrepreneurship and real estate investing with no backup plan.

For the next 2 years, on top of my landlord and real estate adventures, I experimented with both career coaching and content creation, sharing what I learned about being a headhunter to help the general public get ahead in their careers with my career coaching business, Dandan Global.

Setting up DG Recruit

While I enjoyed my time away from recruitment, I realized that (1) very few endeavors in the world pay like recruitment does, and (2) I'd be a fool *not* to establish my own recruiting firm.

This time, I would not only work for myself, but I'd pivot to exclusively service the market I am *most* passionate about, *agency recruitment*!

So in 2018, I established DG Recruit (dgrecruit.com), my recruitment and coaching practice solely dedicated to place agency recruitment professionals at top recruitment agencies. This special niche is called R2R or Rec2Rec, short for recruitment to recruitment (moving people from recruitment firm to recruitment firm).

What makes AR101 a unique and valuable resource is that firstly, I share insider information, key lessons, and tips derived from my personal journey achieving success in the field as a global top biller.

Secondly, I strictly interface and engage with agency recruiters and recruitment owners as an R2R expert, gaining an intimate understanding of the various setups, pay structures, challenges, pros, and cons of recruitment firms of all sizes, nationally and internationally.

In this book, I share with you all the intel I've gathered from both fronts, which makes AR101 the ultimate insider's guide for anyone interested in agency recruitment.

> As you read AR101, stay vigilant for the ⓘ alert. These Insider Insights provide additional information crucial for your journey to gaining a deeper understanding of this business and career.

Reflection on Recruitment

The way I see it is this:

If financial independence is a tree, recruitment is the seed.

Looking back, agency recruitment was the spark that ignited a life of abundance, freedom, and choice.

It was my first, as my dad says, "pot of gold" which kickstarted my wealth creation journey, eventually breaking $1mil in net worth by 30.

Without the money from recruiting, it would've been impossible to buy all the properties I did at such a young age which went on to grow rapidly, continuing to haul more than 6 figures' worth of rental revenue per year. This career has basically set me up for life.

Since recruitment is so entrepreneurial and I own my time being self-employed, I have the luxury and freedom to spend time doing what I enjoy doing, namely R&R (Recruitment and Real estate) along with starting a family, and pursuing other business ventures and hobbies.

As much as work isn't the same thing as being on vacation, I genuinely enjoy my life and work, with agency recruitment as the linchpin of income generation, professional fulfillment, and financial stability.

If I didn't stumble into agency recruitment, I genuinely don't know where or how I could have earned the money I did to get to where I am today.

Spreading the Word!

Having achieved financial freedom so early in life, I feel a deep calling to share information about this business to other motivated and ambitious people searching for a meaningful career and purpose.

As a die-hard economics fan and ethical capitalist, I sincerely believe that if everyone had access to an amazing high earning career like agency recruitment, our world would be a better place.

Leveraging the opportunity in agency recruitment, *anyone* can do amazing things for themselves, their families, and for our world.

Being an agency recruiter gave me critical insights about finances, career strategies, and the consequences of life choices, teaching me through the eyes of my customers how life, business, and careers work from a young age.

The lessons I witnessed firsthand from dealing with a high volume of professionals from junior to C-level on an intimate basis continue to shape me today. Not only did this career create a solid financial foundation that I continue to benefit from, but I also learned so many new and transferable skills to apply to other areas of life and business.

Agency recruitment is financially rewarding, personally fulfilling, and mentally enriching. In hindsight, it equipped me with all the skills and provided the training ground to teach me everything I needed to become a successful entrepreneur.

I would not trade my experiences in this business and career, good *and* bad, for anything! Instead, I feel so grateful and blessed to have found such a great career fit early in life.

This is the core reason why I wrote AR101.

As weird as this sounds, I feel an almost religious fervency to shout from the rooftops for everyone in the world to know that this career exists! It's a prestigious, viable, and enjoyable lifelong profession to grow within while building wealth in a meaningful way.

Now, let's dive into what agency recruitment is all about in the next chapter!

Chapter Highlights:

- Agency recruiters sell candidates to clients and jobs to candidates, earning lucrative commissions.

- Recruitment is a proven pathway to control your income as a niche sales profession; the harder you work, the more effort you expend, the better you are at it, the more you make.

- Earning, saving, and investing combine to create the Wealth Trifecta. The earlier and harder you do this, the faster you can reach FIRE (Financial Independence, Retire Early).

- Investing is key to financial abundance. I chose real estate as my main investment asset class after also experimenting with stocks/equity investing.

- Agency recruitment is financially rewarding and personally fulfilling, making it a prestigious and enjoyable career path.

Recommended Resources:

- If you're interested in learning more about my journey and path to wealth, check out my two podcasts, DG Recruit Podcast (dandanzhu.com/podcasts/dgrecruitpodcast) and Daily DANDAN (dandanzhu.com/podcasts/dailydandan), with plenty of free advice and training on recruitment, investing, life/career strategies, and real estate.

- Check out dandanzhu.com for daily inspiration from the #7777rule blog and to access courses on real estate, recruitment, sales, and personal finance.

CHAPTER 2

WHAT IS AGENCY RECRUITMENT EXACTLY?

When you think of the word "recruiter," what comes to mind?

For some people, "recruiter" invokes an image of a military recruiter they met during high school.

For people who applied to a bunch of internships during college, you may recall an HR or college recruiter vetting you to see if you'd be a good intern or not.

For those of us who are fans of *The Office*, you may conjure up a crystal clear vision of Toby the HR guy. A bit drib, a bit drab, boring, compliance-oriented, and anything but inspiring, charismatic, or exciting of a character.

"Recruitment" is defined as:

The action of finding new people to join an organization.

Due to the breadth of the term, people usually think of one element of recruitment - the HR and internal side of recruiting.

Like most of the general public, I thought recruitment meant internal recruiting and HR.

Even way back when, as a college undergrad majoring in business, I was taught that HR is a function in a company that manages and monitors people's behavior.

These folks are responsible for internal hiring as well as serving as a mediator and overseer of staff and personnel issues. If you stepped out of line, someone would tattle on you to HR and action would be taken.

It was widely accepted that this function and career held no appeal nor garnered prestige or interest in our peer group.

Compared to the exciting opportunities at the Big 4 in accounting/consulting where you got to fly around and work with big brands, investment banking, finance, and other high-paying jobs, recruiting seemed to be the worst option: an unexciting, undesirable, and low-paying career path that was mostly a support function.

It was a last-resort career choice that you'd do simply if you ran out of options. Nobody I knew took any interest in HR or even thought about it as a career track.

We all wanted the big bucks, rewards, and recognition, more commonly found in other career paths.

Little did I know at the time that I was operating ignorantly, only understanding a certain type of recruitment as *agency* recruitment is NOT the same as HR or internal recruiting.

There is a whole other world of recruitment out there, a secret sales career of millionaires, specifically *AGENCY* recruitment.

Agency Recruitment is a Sales Career

Before I became an agency recruiter, I genuinely knew nothing about this business!

Unlike Toby from *The Office* who represents the HR career path, agency recruitment is more like the characters you meet who sell stocks or real estate for a living, making the big bucks, and living lavish lifestyles like you see on *Selling Sunset, Million Dollar Listing,* and *Wolf of Wall Street.*

This profession is a full-on, action-packed, intense, and exciting *sales* career!

What's more interesting is that it's not a one-sided sales transaction as in "sell XYZ product or service to customers". It is actually a *dual-sided* sales job.

This is precisely what differentiates agency recruitment from other sales careers. Unlike traditional sales jobs revolving around selling a tangible product or service in a one-way transaction, agency recruitment requires *two* transactions to result in *one* "sale":

A Business-to-Business (B2B) transaction: Selling recruitment services to clients (companies hiring for open positions)

And

A Business-to-Consumer (B2C) transaction: Selling open positions to candidates (people considering new job opportunities)

B2B		**B2C**
Sell Recruitment Services to Clients		**Sell Roles to Candidates**

In order to conclude in a successful "deal", BOTH need to happen.

If a client does not find the candidate suitable, then the deal is off! Same goes for if the candidate isn't interested in the client's offer or opportunity.

Due to the difficulty of matching these two elements together, the rewards are high for those who are successful at it. In other words, this career is extremely lucrative, *if* you're good at this niche skill.

Both of these "products"—people and jobs—are not your typical product or service, which makes agency recruitment a sales job in a league of its own.

The goal of this professional service is to provide clients with talent and candidates with roles. By "placing" candidates with clients successfully, agency recruitment professionals then receive monetary rewards in the form of placement fees.

Contrary to popular belief, making placements isn't easy!

I've heard people make statements along the lines of "getting people jobs can't be that hard", but many steps go into this intensive process from beginning to end, as covered in Chapter 4.

For a placement to occur, a recruitment agency first needs to secure clients who then provide reqs (job requisitions) for the recruitment agency to work on.

In a classic chicken or egg situation, a recruitment agency cannot survive without both clients AND candidates, thus it's critical to build up clientele on both sides which is referred to in the industry as a book of business.

Success is achieved when an offer (base, bonuses, benefits, etc.) is negotiated and agreed upon by both parties, candidate and client, in a 3-way Win arrangement:

The candidate gets a new (likely more attractive) career opportunity, the client secures their hard-to-find hire, and the agency recruiter earns their lucrative fee.

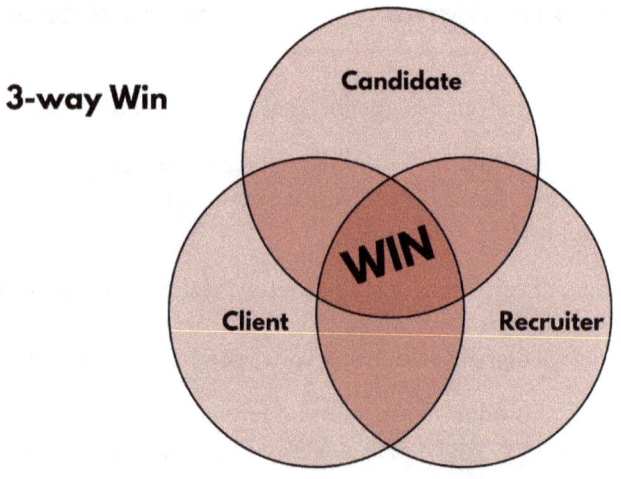

With patience, dedication, and perseverance, top agency recruiters build up their relationships and networks to capture a significant portion of market share to make placements consistently.

Smart companies understand that top talent, many of whom are gainfully employed, do not have the time or incentive to look for new jobs so they engage recruitment agencies to tap into this passive talent pool.

By partnering with experienced recruitment vendors with deep candidate networks, clients can access top talent they otherwise wouldn't have been able to attract through their own means. In return, recruitment agencies get reqs to work on and are rewarded with placement fees.

Ultimately, candidates win the most in this setup!

That's why there's a strong incentive for candidates to align with top recruitment agencies in their market instead of applying directly to companies hiring. Since employers pay the recruitment fee, candidates receive career and job search support for free and can negotiate better compensation packages going through agency recruiters.

This cycle of win-win-win can last indefinitely as the relationships between great agency recruiters and their clients and candidates can stretch for many years and sometimes, entire careers.

Why Recruitment Agencies Exist

If agency recruitment fees are so high, why do companies use them? Wouldn't it be cheaper to hire candidates directly without the use of recruitment partners?

Also, why do companies have to pay recruitment fees when people want to find jobs on their own?

The reality is that many companies are not hurting for money as much as they need hard-to-find talent. While not all can afford to utilize recruitment firms, those who can, do. It's the fastest and most efficient way to solve acute talent gaps.

Companies need qualified staff to run their business, and most industries have a shortage of qualified labor, which come together to drive demand for specialist recruitment services. Recruitment agencies smartly capitalize on commercial opportunities in candidate-dry market niches in fields such as STEM (Science, Technology, Engineering, and Mathematics) and many others.

For certain high profile, confidential, specialist, and/or critical roles, companies can't afford to hire someone who isn't vetted and qualified as a guaranteed top hire. Plus, the candidates responding to the job ads are often not a fit so clients would rather spend money on recruitment partners whose sole job is to solicit and secure better applicants.

Many clients have experienced that the financial consequences of bad hires costs the company more than the recruitment fee would've been! In a way, partnering with a well-known, highly respected agency recruiter provides insurance that the hire will likely be of a higher caliber than the candidates the internal recruitment team presents.

Furthermore, candidates *themselves* may not feel comfortable responding to a company's direct solicitation to poach them from their current employer. Recruitment agencies, because they're a 3rd party, can jump in to become that bridge to build trust over time.

More passive candidates (candidates who aren't actively looking for a role) feel comfortable interacting with recruitment agencies instead of directly applying to a firm.

Although it's cheaper to hire without engaging a recruitment agency, it doesn't result in hiring the right person for a number of specialty roles where it takes a real industry insider to judge talent accurately. Therefore, employers don't mind (and have no choice) but to pay a premium for external support on critical hires in select career tracks.

The US is an extremely competitive labor market (more on this in Chapter 3), so top candidates have multiple options to choose from.

The competitive advantage of hiring the *right* people is many times more than the associated hiring costs. Firms are willing to shell out recruitment fees to capture the best candidates because they know the price they pay is peanuts compared to the commercial value top hires bring to the table.

Without the right people in place, companies can't successfully grow and achieve their business objectives which is why recruiting top talent is such a priority and non-negotiable need for every organization.

There are two main types of recruitment: direct hire and staffing (further broken down in Chapters 5 and 6, respectively).

Direct hire is when a firm hires a candidate as a full-time employee. Staffing is when a company brings on additional labor support by hiring contractors/temp workers. Some recruitment agencies may provide both temp and perm recruitment services, while some primarily service one or the other.

Another reason why companies may engage with a recruitment agency is to replace some of their current staff with higher quality candidates in a confidential search. This helps companies reduce disruption due to disgruntled or worried internal staff around job security.

Recruitment is a versatile pay-to-play model that helps solve any and all hiring needs that arise!

Recruitment Agencies are Selective

Remember Toby the HR guy from *The Office*? His responsibility is to hire for internal teams but often he isn't successful in filling every role.

In some cases, there aren't many qualified candidates and those who are, don't need a job since they're already actively working. In markets like these, there are not enough qualified candidates to go around, so the role becomes extremely hard to fill. That's when companies engage external recruitment agencies to help.

Since recruitment agencies charge a hefty fee, a key expectation is that agency recruiters are going to be better at securing top quality candidates for their clients. If a role were easy to fill, there would be no need to pay a fee to an external recruitment agency because it can be covered by internal recruiters at no extra cost.

When recruitment firms partner to augment internal recruitment efforts, recruitment firms have to work hard to unearth top candidates in order to justify their fee.

This means, agency recruiters have to be adept salespeople and interviewers, prescient and knowledgeable in their market specialism in order to present appropriately qualified candidates to their clients.

Furthermore, recruiters are competing against other agencies for market share, so they have to work extremely hard to position themselves as *the* go-to connector for the best and brightest candidates to win searches from clients.

As a recruiter, you're only as good as your product aka your candidate(s). Along this vein, if you consistently try to advocate for less desirable candidates, clients will start to distrust your capability to judge candidate quality well!

Thus, the harsh reality of this job is that it's not for someone who wants to help unsuitable candidates down on their luck. In this business, the strong align with the strong.

As true agency recruiters love to remind others, it's not a social services role or a particularly charitable job. Unlike unemployment offices and job outplacement companies, this business is not for bleeding hearts who want to help downtrodden people.

Don't get me wrong—recruitment agencies help candidates and clients as a natural byproduct resulting from making successful placements.

However, helping people is a byproduct of being driven to excel. Don't forget, it is a fully for-profit, and dare I say, profit-first, monetization model of selling placeable candidates for a fee that influences agency recruiters' best practices, incentives, and behaviors.

In most recruitment markets, you're servicing top clients paying top dollar for you to search high and low for the sharpest, most desirable candidates in that particular niche. These candidates are often gainfully employed, highly paid, and *not* in need of a job change.

To crack into the network of the candidates your clients eagerly want to hire, you have to be reputable, engaging, clever, persistent, and charming (more traits of top billers explained in Chapter 10).

The goal is to somehow persuade them to take a new job with one of your clients, ideally sooner rather than later. To move a candidate in such a powerfully privileged position, you have to painstakingly build relationships to win their trust over time, then inspire them to take action, a process which may require months or years to actualize!

In other words, you have to be patient, persevere, and work hard to succeed in this line of work.

Agency Recruitment Pros and Cons

Agency recruitment is one of the most profitable business models I have ever witnessed, compared to other industries where margins are razor thin and operating overheads are constantly climbing.

Other than a computer, internet connection, phone, and other industry-specific tools discussed in Chapter 11, some basic legal and accounting startup fees, and most importantly, the knowledge of how to run a recruitment desk, there aren't many other fixed or variable costs initially to get a direct hire* recruitment practice up and running.

*Staffing firms are more capital-intensive initially but the potential profit margins and residual revenues more than make up for the higher setup costs. Chapter 6 dives deeply into why this is the case.

Many agency recruiters are fully remote so even renting an office is not necessary! And unlike lawyers, recruiters aren't burdened with law school debt, don't need to pass tests, and are not required to obtain licenses and credentialing to start practicing.

Furthermore, from a regulatory standpoint, there are no governing bodies controlling what recruitment agencies can or cannot do, other than General Data Protection Regulation (GDPR) laws, only enforceable and applicable to businesses operating in the European Union (EU).

In the USA, there is only one regulation that is in effect only for certain states which limits recruiters from asking candidates how much money they're currently making.

Thus, especially in the USA, compared to other sales jobs with heavy regulatory oversight (realtors, medical device/drug sales, financial wealth sales, etc.), the freedom agency recruiters have is unparalleled.

This allows agency recruiters to run their practice with marketing creativity and personal flexibility with reduced worry and legal liability.

For many of these reasons, agency recruitment is such an interesting and exciting industry that provides enterprising individuals with an advantageous opportunity to make their mark and earn a lucrative living.

However, the drawback to this profession is that it's actually really hard to excel at and master!

Because of the lack of regulation, the barriers to entry are low, which leads to high volumes of people coming into the business and unfortunately, failing.

Although recruitment appears straightforward on the surface, in actuality, only a small portion of recruitment professionals survive and thrive.

The industry's high turnover rate makes the competition weak and reliable recruiters scarce. Thus, those who *do* make it, achieve significant success relatively quickly.

The more effective, ethical, and persistent the agency recruiter is, the more business they will receive through referrals because their reputation precedes them.

Unlike other sales careers that are more transactional, agency recruiters have to work hard to uphold their industry reputation because customer networks are insular, well-connected, and limited in size, where word gets around quickly.

Chapter Highlights:

- Agency recruitment is a unique sales role requiring two sales transactions to result in one placement: Selling Candidates to Clients (B2B) and Selling Roles to Candidates (B2C).

- Companies engage recruitment agencies to find hard-to-find talent quickly and efficiently, especially in candidate-dry market niches.

- There are two main types of recruitment: direct hire (full-time employment) and staffing (contract/temporary labor).

- Recruitment agencies are expected to provide top quality candidates to justify their fees, making the job demanding but rewarding.

- Agency recruitment offers a lucrative business model with low barriers to entry and little-to-no regulation.

- Recruitment agencies' priority is to generate as much profit as possible by servicing only the top companies and candidates in their niche(s).

- This is a competitive business, not to be confused with career coaching and outplacement companies who help unemployed people down on their luck find jobs or pivot careers.

- Successful agency recruiters receive referrals through word-of-mouth marketing, maintaining their reputation and expanding their business.

- Unlike other sales jobs, agency recruiters must uphold high ethical standards due to their niche focus and reliance on reputation.

CHAPTER 3

THE AGENCY RECRUITMENT MARKET

Agency recruitment exists in every country and every sector. Within the agency recruitment space, there are firms of various types and sizes.

Let's start by examining large and midsize recruitment firms, where many agency recruiters start their career at.

Large and Midsize Recruitment Firms

In many industries, large firms who employ a significant amount of staff have robust training and development programs to support entry-level hires. Starting one's career at such a firm is a typical rite of passage for many professionals.

The same phenomenon occurs in recruitment, where large and midsize recruitment firms hire and train big numbers of new recruiters, typically right after they graduate from college or a few years out of school.

Similar to other industries like law or consulting, the sheer hiring power and financial backing of big firms usually exceeds the hiring volume that smaller firms can support.

International and national recruitment firms vary significantly in their growth strategies and go-to-market approaches. Some of the biggest recruitment agencies have up to 60k staff worldwide. However, most big recruitment firms are primarily US-based with national staff numbers ranging from 10k-20k while midsize recruiting firms employ a few hundred to a few thousand internal staff.

Since agency recruitment is a meritocratic profession, recruiters who hit strong billing numbers are promoted rapidly and paid much more than their peers. They access career advancement faster than what's possible in other careers that are less dependent on revenue generation.

For top billers working at large and midsize global firms, opportunities to advance are plentiful. Top performers can elect to continue in their current position, move up into a management role, join another team, or set up their own division in a new region and/or abroad.

Large and midsize recruitment firms are generally structured and bureaucratic for multiple reasons. Because their model revolves around upskilling entry-level recruiters, they need to manage their staff by strictly monitoring key performance indicators (KPIs).

KPIs are targets that recruiters are expected to hit or beat. In many sales careers, KPIs are set for every producer to ensure certain volumes of activity are being completed which hopefully will result in deals over time.

If KPIs aren't being met, performance improvement plans (PIPs) are deployed in order to get the producer back on track. If they fail to rectify their activity levels and expend more effort, they'll likely be let go from the organization as sales businesses cannot keep carrying non-performers or underperformers.

This leads to high overhead costs per staff member both managerially as well as systemically. The base salaries, benefits provided, office rent expenses, training resources, management oversight needed, and back-office operations cost quite a bit of money to maintain.

The hope is that every hire will start earning money for the firm to pay back the overhead costs of employing and training them up. However, in reality, few become exceptional performers and turnover remains high at these large and midsize recruitment firms.

Complicating matters even more, many large and midsize recruitment firms may elect to sell a portion of their business to investment firms or go public. This decision often stems from the desire of senior leaders and founding teams to cash out on the firm's value and gain further financial rewards.

As a result, recruitment companies frequently engage in mergers, acquisitions, and accept outside investments to fuel growth. However, these actions come with expectations from shareholders, investors, and backers, pressuring teams to rapidly expand revenues and team sizes, sometimes at the expense of hiring standards.

This high-pressure, competitive, and micromanaged environment may cause successful top billers to outgrow the company over time. Without sufficient financial incentives to stay, they may choose to leave, seeking opportunities at smaller, boutique recruitment firms.

Boutique Recruitment Firms

Boutique recruitment firms are much smaller organizations where headcount can be as low as 5 people up to a few hundred, which is why they're attractive to top billers coming from larger agencies who want more space to grow and power to influence.

Because boutique agencies tend to be privately owned and independently operated without outside influence, smaller recruitment businesses are markedly different from large and midsize recruiting firms.

They can offer more bespoke opportunities for their internal staff and their clients and candidates as they're more flexible with less internal bureaucracy and limitations.

Plus, they're not forced to grow for the sake of growing in order to live up to outside investors' unrealistic expectations, something many large recruitment firms can't ignore.

Another big difference is this:

Agency recruiters working at boutique firms usually have more of a blank slate to do as they see fit with less internal competition. That way, recruiters are building their networks together, not against each other.

With less staff in each region, there could be more collaboration amongst recruiters to share candidates and clients unlike at bigger firms where ownership rules are more stringent and inflexible.

This isn't to say that all boutiques run perfectly or are by default better than large and midsize recruitment firms!

There are many boutique firms that *also* promote toxic leaders and cultures which inhibits their ability to attract new hires and grow their headcount. They may be just as likely to suffer from high turnover and eventual failure.

Thus, it's important to consider whether the firm is a boutique by design or may be struggling to grow due to persistent internal issues.

This is why researching the founders and team members through careful vetting when selecting which firm to join is so critical as I'll cover in Chapter 12.

Lastly, since most boutiques aren't set up to deliver training and development programs en masse to hiring classes, they tend to hire experienced recruitment talent who come out of large and midsize recruitment firms.

The International Market

Because agency recruitment is a global industry, successful billers can opt to take their recruitment career internationally!

For example, many UK and/or European recruitment agencies have expanded into Dubai, Asian, and Latin American markets due to favorable tax terms, attractive commercial incentives, and acceptance of using English within business settings.

As more countries' economies and labor markets develop, their recruitment markets grow in tandem. New frontiers and markets are proliferating as many countries experience rapid modernization, economic expansion, material and commercial abundance, and innovation.

Thus, the opportunity within this career is at an early stage with enormous future potential and without limits to growth!

The most marked expansion pattern is UK recruitment firms coming to the USA (and Australian firms to a much smaller extent) due to the E-2/E-3 Visa and Trade pact, which deserves its own segment, coming up next.

UK Recruitment Firms

In 1945 (and amended in 1993), the US-UK Treaty of Friendship, Commerce, and Navigation was signed which allows for certain categories of UK nationals, including investors and business owners, to apply for E-2 visas to come to the US to invest "substantially" by establishing a domestic footprint.

Due to this treaty, many UK businesses, especially recruitment agencies, have moved to the US to take advantage of the strong economy that dwarfs their domestic opportunities.

Because headhunters who can meet clients and candidates in person have a higher chance of building strong and lasting relationships, it's worth it for agencies to expand their physical presence in the geographic markets they serve in order to acquire and retain market share.

While many UK firms can recruit US talent from their offices in the UK, many UK firms chose to partake in the E-2 visa program to physically relocate key personnel to the USA, gaining a boots on the ground competitive advantage.

Given the mature and highly competitive recruitment landscape in the UK, which has honed its expertise in the field since the post-WWII era, UK recruiters stand as true masters of the trade. Their experience of perfecting their craft over generations make them exceptionally experienced, proficient, and adept at building profitable recruitment practices.

As they extend their reach into the relatively nascent recruitment market of the USA, this advantage provides them with a substantial headstart, resulting in high profits that, in turn, fuel their rapid expansion into new offices and territories.

Due to this phenomenon, a strong and formidable presence of UK recruitment agencies developed in the US since the mid 2000s with remarkable success, now employing large numbers of both UK nationals and American personnel.

While anything is subject to change in the future, as of this writing in 2023, these factors make the American recruitment opportunity undeniably one of the best, if not THE best:

1. **The strong US currency.**

The US dollar (USD) is still the world's reserve currency. Until this changes, the US remains a top recruitment market.

Compared to other currencies that have experienced more volatility and recent devaluation, the USD has not only remained strong but gained ground. Therefore, recruitment firms charging and earning in dollars are winning already off of the exchange rate alone.

2. **Salaries in the US are *the* highest, leading to higher fees.**

Because the US is more capitalistic, salaries are higher due to lower social benefits. Workers primarily rely on their income to survive which leads to the US having the highest salaries across the board.

Since recruitment fees are charged as a percentage of compensation (more on this in Chapter 5), billing off of high salaries mathematically leads to high placement fees.

This is especially the case in niche STEM markets facing labor shortages, the exact niches recruitment firms exist to cater to. Average deal sizes in the USA combined with the power of the USD end up being *higher* than other countries' placement fees by significant amounts.

Considering executive compensation in the US continues to break global records, executive search placement fees are especially impressive, by far outstripping any placement fee achievable in other countries. It may take years, possibly decades, for other markets to catch up.

3. US recruitment fee percentages remain high.

Not only are salaries high in the US, recruitment firms can sustainably sell their services at a higher percentage than what's possible in other countries.

Because agency recruitment is still a nascent industry in the US and the market is so big, the saturation point has not yet been met, nor will it be for quite some time to come. This keeps placement fee percentages persistently high, a great thing for recruitment agencies.

Unlike other markets, specifically the UK, where recruitment is a more mature industry with companies fighting against each other in a race to the bottom, recruitment fee percentages in the US remain attractive and high.

For example, 10%-20% fees are more common in the UK due to intense competition driving rates down while top agencies in the US can regularly charge 20%-35% fees. What a world of a difference!

4. The USA is rife with commercial opportunity.

As one of the strongest economies in the world with a healthy and highly promising trajectory across all industries spanning a large geographic territory to boot, the commercial opportunity in the USA is favorable to recruitment firms.

The startup scene and overall capitalistic environment of the USA benefits recruiters massively. Firms need to woo talent from their competitors by any means necessary which is exactly why agency recruitment services exist!

While global growth has been astronomical with developing countries making exponential leaps of innovation, the USA remains a staple and stable economic power.

Furthermore, the strength of the legal system, infrastructure, and affordable technology tools/resources available makes commercial activity safe and sustainable. As companies grow, naturally, they need to hire, a boon for recruitment firms.

5. **Lastly, American workers are culturally attuned to change jobs.**

Given the prevalent at-will employment structure, it's common and socially acceptable for American workers to move firms freely.

As cultural norms have shifted over the last few generations, nowadays professionals switch firms much more frequently, breeding opportunities for headhunters to profit from each career move.

Since workers typically receive bigger compensation increases when moving employers instead of receiving a low cost of living adjustment per year should they choose to remain at their existing employer, the financial incentive to leverage headhunters' services to obtain a new job is high.

Some headhunters do such a great job of staying in touch with their network that they'll place a candidate multiple times!

Unlike markets where moving jobs is considered shameful or otherwise socially frowned upon (common in countries like Japan where employers hold more power culturally), switching jobs in the US is very much an accepted societal norm.

These reasons, among many, are why recruiters from all over the world come to the US to seek their recruitment fortunes. If their strategy and execution is effective, they can quickly make an impact on the market and reap a strong return on investment (ROI).

To further illustrate this point, the commercial opportunity in the US is so lucrative that the US division often rapidly becomes the highest-grossing entity within many international recruitment firms, within 1-2 short years.

Since the 2000s and especially after the 2009 financial crisis, many UK firms established offices across the USA to grow their profits abroad. I started my career as one of the first American hires at one of the most famous UK agencies that became the poster child of successful international expansion.

Many other UK firms followed suit around the same timeframe with similar training, market approaches, compensation plans, and internal culture, also reaching significant levels of success with accelerated growth of 20-300% per year in headcount.

This trajectory of UK firms doing well in the USA doesn't seem to be slowing down any time soon! They've since become integrated into the US economic fabric and recruitment scene, undeniably important as a hiring force as they continue to develop many entry-level recruiters into future stars.

If you're looking into recruitment jobs, you'll inevitably encounter UK recruitment businesses as a potential place to launch your career. They are certainly worth considering.

Foreign Recruitment Firms & Vendors

Outside of UK recruitment firms who are the primary non-American firms operating in the US, recruiters based in India, the Philippines, Asia, and Latin America are *all* working roles in the US market despite being based abroad.

Instead of relocating here due to prohibitive US immigration laws, they prospect and sell to US-based businesses during US working hours from their local region.

They're completely within their rights to do so! Foreign recruitment companies can solicit US clients freely. The US government, business environment, and laws cannot stop this from happening as there are no regulations requiring certification or licensing to operate a recruitment firm of any type.

Due to the attractive elements of the US market previously mentioned, recruitment firms, services, vendors, and outsourced functions offered by businesses based abroad are eager to get a piece of the American pie.

If they can land just one client, they can earn in USD while living and working in their home countries. This allows them to profit off of currency arbitrage while providing lower cost solutions to clients in an effort to win market share.

It has become increasingly common to see services and businesses headquartered abroad targeting US clients or partnering with US recruitment firms to outsource certain tasks.

For companies looking to save costs on hiring US-based staff, they may choose to leverage these outsourcing/offshoring service providers.

Like many elements of the recruitment industry, this is newer territory as companies learn and experiment on how to best partner with international businesses to run their recruitment operations.

Some recruitment agencies may choose to leverage this option heavily while some use outsourced services minimally to never. Every firm operates in a way that best aligns with their comfort level and business strategy.

Chapter Highlights:

- The agency recruitment business exists worldwide, with various types and sizes of firms in every country and sector.

- Many agency recruiters start their career at large and midsize recruitment firms due to the robust training and development programs for entry-level hires they offer.

- Boutique recruitment firms offer more flexibility and opportunities for top billers, but they may also face internal issues hindering growth.

- The international market presents significant opportunities for successful recruiters to take their career abroad (immigration laws permitting).

- UK recruitment firms have expanded to the USA due to favorable treaties, resulting in a formidable presence in the American market.

- The US recruitment market is the strongest due to a variety of factors (currency, commercial environment, fee structure, rates, etc.) which is why firms from all over the world have either expanded to the US physically or target the US despite being based abroad.

- UK firms have succeeded in the USA due to their sharp recruitment skills coming from a mature and competitive market which has provided a huge benefit that many UK firms are taking advantage of to this day. They are now a powerful employer contingent in the US for entry-level and experienced recruiters alike.

CHAPTER 4

THE AGENCY RECRUITMENT PROCESS

Recruitment is an art *and* a science. Making placements resembles an iceberg; there's much more going on under the surface than meets the eye!

As you can see, a lot of effort, training, hard work, and consistency goes into building a thriving and profitable recruitment business.

In fact, more commonly than not, many people underestimate just how hard this job actually is!

The simplistic mindset of "how hard can it be?" combined with greed for fast and easy money often results in eventual failure. Many people are completely unprepared and ill-equipped to face the immense challenges that inevitably arise during the recruitment process.

Furthermore, it doesn't help that many irresponsible "gurus" tout recruitment (or any trending side hustle) as being "easy".

Having lived this career and business, I can assure you:

Agency recruitment is not a get-rich-quick (and easy!) scheme.

Quick and easy deals are exceptions to the rule. Most placements are tough and difficult, unearthing a bevy of issues and landmines that you must navigate through.

Unfortunately, there is nothing stopping people from flippantly undermining our industry and giving it a bad name, hurting many people in the process.

More outrageously so, many marketers, social media trainers, and lead generation scam artists sell themselves as experts on recruitment when they've never done a single placement in their lives.

We insiders know though:

You can't AI, machine learn, lead generate, email drip, or manipulate your way into running a top agency. If this business were so simple, why, everyone would be a millionaire!

The opposite is true: very few people actually reach the pinnacle of success in this profession.

The process of becoming an elite professional in our line of work requires practice, unwavering effort, and years of study.

Even though it's technically possible for anyone to open a recruitment business with no formal prior training because it's an unregulated industry requiring zero credentialing, it's quite difficult for people with no previous hands-on experience to consistently make placements.

This is why it's rare that recruitment agencies founded by novices succeed in the mid to long term. Generally, most founders got their start by working for someone else where they learned the ins and outs of the business.

Let's break down how the agency recruitment process works in more detail, starting with the client side.

The Agency Recruitment Process

1. Business Development
2. Solidify Terms, Process, Parameters
3. Recruiting Candidates
4. Submit Profiles
5. Manage Interview Processes
6. Offer Negotiation
7. Secure Offer Acceptance
8. Candidate Starts
9. Client Pays
10. Guarantee Period Passed!

Step 1: Business Development

The first step of the agency recruitment process is to negotiate and agree to commercial and legal contract terms with clients in a sales process called BD (business development).

After all, it's a moot point if you don't have clients to pay you for your recruitment services!

Thus, recruiters must sell their services and capabilities to hiring managers, decision-makers who have the power to decide which candidates to hire.

Building a client book is often seen as one of the most difficult and daunting aspects of this job as you're competing against fierce competitors to win market share.

Starting out, agency recruiters have to spend an inordinate amount of their time prospecting. They utilize a variety of methods including cold calling, email marketing campaigns, LinkedIn messaging, referrals, in-person networking events and conferences, wining and dining, leveraging social media, text message engagement, etc.

In addition to these traditional BD efforts, salespeople also host, sponsor, or attend in-person and virtual events, conferences, expert panels, and webinars to build clientele. Overall, the sky's the limit here in the variety of options you can consider to implement in your BD strategy!

While these expenditures aren't cheap at the outset, they more than cover their cost when recruitment agencies are able to drive brand awareness, woo clients, build customer loyalty, and win searches through these efforts.

Whether or not firms already have an established book of clients, agency recruiters still must fight hard to attract more because nothing is guaranteed in recruitment.

A key client may suddenly stop hiring, prompting recruitment firms to scramble and find new clients to service. As market conditions can change on a dime, BD remains a core function to keep any recruitment business profitable.

BD approaches vary depending on the current landscape and the agency's market standing. Companies who've had longer term success in certain niches benefit from a competitive advantage due to track record and longevity of relationships, while others newer on the scene must work harder to prove themselves.

Regardless of market standing, all recruitment firms must preemptively pipeline future business to hedge against any potential hiring freezes or slowdowns within their existing client base.

Once you have a potential client on the line, you have to handle tough conversations on the fly. Agency recruitment professionals must speak credibly about their market expertise in a way that assures clients that they're indeed Subject Matter Experts (SMEs) who are best positioned to fill their reqs.

Because the majority of business development is done by phone or video calls, it's critical to carry yourself in a professional manner so clients know that they can trust you with their business. For the most part, this is primarily a telesales job with little face-to-face interaction outside of in-person meetings and events that come up.

While the BD process is daunting, with courage, confidence, and persistent hard work, many enterprising entry-level recruiters have succeeded in building phenomenal client relationships that result in breaking key accounts and billing records.

Step 2: Solidify Terms, Process, and Parameters

As with most professional services, it is critical to agree on business terms and conditions (T&Cs) before recruitment efforts commence. Every client has their own idiosyncrasies and comfort levels of what they will agree to.

Thus, agency recruiters need to negotiate and agree on contract terms with each client, including solidifying language around these common clauses, not limited to the following:

- The engagement/search details
- The placement fee percentage the agency will receive
- What the fee percentage is charged on
- When the agency will be paid
- What happens if the placement doesn't work out
- The interview process flow
- Timelines both parties will adhere to
- What counts as a valid candidate submission
- Candidate ownership periods*
- Retained or contingent search processes

*Candidate ownership periods are important because if a candidate applies to the company directly, through another recruitment agency, or engages with any internal member employed by the client such as an HR professional or a hiring manager, the recruitment agency may not re-represent or re-submit the candidate's profile for a certain amount of time (usually 6 months to 1 year). This is to prevent duplicate submissions of the candidate, eliminating the client's risk of being forced to pay out an extra recruitment fee.

> ① *In Chapter 5, I will cover all the details and differences of how retained and contingent searches work. However, as most searches are done on a contingent basis, this chapter describes how typical contingent search processes work, where the fee is paid out upon the candidate being successfully identified, processed, and placed, instead of being required upfront to start the search like in a retained setup.*

Many clients expect recruitment firms to capitulate to *their* contract terms in order to land a coveted spot on the PSL (preferred suppliers' list). This special list officially approves recruitment firms to partner.

On the other hand, some clients may be receptive to adopting the contract terms proposed by recruitment firms rather than imposing their own terms.

Either way, both the recruitment agency and client should ideally agree to contract terms and officially sign these documents in advance of providing services.

Skipping this step poses a potential risk as the client may refuse to pay the fee if the recruitment company was not formally authorized to partner with them on searches.

Without legally binding contractual agreements in place, clients may not feel obliged to compensate for the recruitment services they received.

Therefore, it's best practice to agree to and sign off on contract terms *before* the placement process progresses too far ahead.

> ① *If clients are not willing to pay the recruitment fee, then you clearly cannot align and partner with them as agency recruitment is a pay-to-play professional service; it is not a free service.*
>
> *Just like a lawyer cannot give pro-bono advice to businesses in order to run a successful law firm, recruitment agencies similarly need to make a living charging for their time, efforts, and services. This is why contracts need to be negotiated, agreed to, and signed, earlier rather than later.*

Once contracts are solidified, the recruitment firm works with the client to clarify the details, parameters, and requirements of the search, including but not limited to:

- What the role entails such as titles, responsibilities, candidate seniority, expectations
- The setup the job requires whether on-site, off-site, hybrid, or remote
- Salary bands and compensation components
- Technical and soft skills the ideal candidate must have
- Which firms to recruit from, which firms to avoid
- What tools, perks, and corporate benefits candidates can expect to receive
- Detailed rundown of interview processes, submission process, logistics to arrange interviews, assessments required, and timelines for each step
- Any and all other information relevant to help candidates understand the opportunity and job offering more

Now that everything is agreed upon, the recruitment agency has all they need to proceed to the next step of the recruitment process.

Step 3: Recruiting Candidates

Once the req is secured, now is the time to fill it!

Armed with all the information about the role, the recruiter can start recruiting candidates.

Whether through LinkedIn, job boards, cold calling, responses to advertisements, or their own database of candidates, recruiters must hustle to identify, source, engage, and interview active and passive candidates who may qualify for the req at hand.

The more creative your candidate engagement efforts and the harder you work, the more success you'll have in finding the ideal candidate clients want, the proverbial needle in the haystack.

Related to this point, the onus lies on the recruiter to market themselves and their open reqs using their own ingenuity and creativity as most recruitment firms offer little to no marketing support, especially when it comes to social media, an emerging tool many recruiters are using to great results.

Recruiters who have taken the initiative to create content pieces like posts, videos, interviews, and articles for self-promotion on social media such as LinkedIn, have built up large social media followings which helps them recruit candidates and attract clients alike.

Contrary to outdated thinking that phone conversations are the crux of this sales business, there is no debate that strong social media marketing efforts translate into tangible commercial value!

This is because candidates and clients who feel familiar with top headhunters' marketing are more likely to reach out to and respond to them *first*, giving them a massive competitive edge to win customers' allegiance ahead of competitors.

Social media for recruitment firms is still in its infancy as most recruiters are blind and stubbornly resistant to the power of this marketing channel. While it doesn't matter as much in the immediate short term, social media followings will make a huge difference in the next 5 -10 years. Mark my words.

> ① *We've also created a Social Media Course for Recruitment firms and professionals you can take at dgrecruit.com/courses that teaches you how to replicate our success in leveraging social media to build our recruitment practice.*

All of this being said, catching the candidates' attention to connect and engage is only part of the equation.

More importantly, recruiting suitable candidates relies on agency recruiters' skills to assess each discussion and interview thoroughly to read the situation correctly.

Volume-wise, there is an urgency to present enough candidates within an acceptable time frame so the client can commence interviewing.

This is why recruitment is a sales job; agency recruiters have to sell the role effectively to as many qualified people as possible in order to increase the odds of presenting multiple candidates and filling the req promptly.

Since there are so many different life and career scenarios that may complicate candidates' ability to move companies, careful thought goes into each conversation to make sure it's worth everyone's time to formally proceed to the next stage of the recruitment process.

Step 4: Submit Profiles

Once the candidates are fully committed to moving forward with the process, the recruiter then needs to gather information and documents in order to formally submit the candidate profile to the client.

This includes obtaining the candidate's resume and disclosing pertinent details such as salary needs, candidate background, career highlights, justifications on why the candidate may be an appropriate hire, reason for leaving, and potential timelines.

Recruiters then compile and send a detailed writeup summarizing everything to the client via email with any accompanying attachments.

In some cases, clients may request recruitment vendors to submit candidate information directly through a website specifically geared towards tracking candidate submissions from external partners.

Every client has different processes and demands so it's critical to keep detailed notes on each client in order to comply with submission guidelines and protocols.

Step 5: Manage Interview Processes

Once candidates are submitted, it's up to the client to decide if they're interested to proceed or not.

If the client selects a candidate to interview, the recruitment agency or the client's internal team then schedules and confirms interview logistics with both parties.

Some clients prefer a more hands-on approach from their agency partners, whereas others prefer to fully take over interview and debrief processes with minimal engagement from their agency partner henceforth.

In either case, clients are motivated to woo top talent into their ranks so they support interview processes on scheduling as well as selling the opportunity in a positive manner to win candidates over.

When interviews at each stage have concluded, the recruiter and client discuss feedback to decide if there is further interest to proceed to later stage interviews or an offer.

Simultaneously, the agency recruiter also communicates with the candidate to gauge their feedback and interest level in the opportunity.

Because this is such a high touch and high stakes stage of the recruitment life cycle, this is the most time consuming part of the process.

Even waiting for interviews to occur could take quite some time as many are scheduled far in advance. Thus, it's the agency recruiter's job to stay in touch with everyone before, during, and after interviews to keep everyone engaged.

At any given point in the process, the agency recruiter can follow up with and/or further advocate for the candidate or client if there seems to be hesitation.

As the go-between, agency recruiters have significant power to influence both parties. Recruiters who are good at this are so effective that they consistently alter the outcome of the recruitment process in their favor, resulting in more success.

While many feedback loops may progress smoothly, there are times where clients and candidates may misunderstand each other. When miscommunication occurs, it's imperative for the agency recruiter to set the record straight as advocates, troubleshooters, negotiators, and problem solvers for both parties.

Step 6: Offer Negotiation

After the interviews are completed and the client has chosen the candidate they want to hire, the recruiter provides additional support in negotiating the specific offer details including but not limited to:

- Title the offer will reflect
- Base, bonus, stocks, options offered
- Expected start date
- What benefits are provided such as 401k match, healthcare plan, and paid time off (PTO) policy

Some candidates may prioritize certain elements of the offer over others. Therefore, it's the recruiter's responsibility to communicate and align both parties' expectations, increasing the chances of the client presenting an attractive package that will be accepted.

The offer negotiation process could be smooth, quick, and easy. Conversely, this step can get complicated, dicey, and actually fall apart!

In either scenario, the recruiter plays a huge part in working out the kinks, salvaging what can be saved, and coming up with creative means to rescue the deal. If that's not possible, then it's back to the drawing board or maybe the search is off.

In the ideal outcome that a suitable candidate is identified and reciprocates interest in the role, the recruiter negotiates an offer with parameters the candidate is likely to accept and the placement process continues.

Step 7: Secure Offer Acceptance

Once the recruiter and client cavort to discuss what conditions the candidate is interested to accept within the formal offer, it's time to generate the formal offer paperwork.

Sometimes, the recruitment firm receives the formal offer in its entirety to present to the candidate, answering any questions along the way and obtaining signatures to send back to the client.

However, just as often, clients may want to take over at this stage and deliver the formal offer directly to the candidate either through their HR representative who will then help with next steps and onboarding or through the hiring manager who warmly welcomes the new hire to the team.

This is completely dependent on the client's protocol and also the client/recruiter relationship. In both cases, the recruiter remains ready to support as needed to secure the candidate's acceptance.

Should either party need the recruiter's continued support, they jump right back into the fray to troubleshoot and handle any unforeseen issues that may arise.

Once the offer is agreed upon and no further negotiation is needed, both parties sign the official offer and confirm the start date, concluding and closing out the search formally.

Step 8: Candidate Starts

Just because the offer is accepted doesn't mean the process is over yet! The recruiter is responsible to ensure that the candidate follows through to successfully start their new role.

If the candidate does not show up for work, the deal is off the table. In these cases, they're called a dropper or a fall-off (as in the candidate dropped out of work).

This is a recruiter's worst nightmare. Blame may be assigned to the recruitment firm and cause the client to lose trust in the recruiter.

Thankfully, in the majority of cases, this doesn't happen! Most candidates will start their job without incident.

Customarily, agency recruiters will wish their candidates a successful start and touch base in a timely manner to make sure everything goes off without a hitch.

Step 9: Guarantee Period Passed

Even if the candidate starts, the recruitment fee is still not secure!

The client could fire the placed candidate for incompetence, over exaggerating capabilities, bad performance, inappropriate behavior at work, or lack of culture fit.

Similarly, the candidate could quit due to the workplace environment being toxic, safety concerns, ethical challenges, or the manager being difficult and uncooperative.

Regardless of the validity of why the placement didn't work out, the client may be entitled to a full/partial fee refund or the placement fee may be credited and applied to future placements' invoices if the candidate "drops" within a certain time period.

The period in which a client could be eligible for this sort of rebate or refund is commonly referred to as a "guarantee" or "rebate" period. This guarantee period is usually an industry standard of 90 days, however some contracts may have clauses ranging from 30 days to 1 year.

As with everything in recruitment, nothing is static or uniform. Since labor markets operate so differently, certain market niches may require longer or shorter guarantee time frames.

Since the fees recruitment agencies charge are so high, clients protect themselves financially with this clause, something most recruitment contracts are bound to cover.

Suffering the financial consequences of a dropper could be devastating due to the time, effort, and energy invested into a deal that results in lost revenue to the firm and lost commission income to the recruiter.

Thus, it's imperative for recruitment agencies to train their staff well on best practices when it comes to contract negotiation to protect their own interests down the line.

As an example, recruitment contracts might specify situations in which a refund or credit would not be issued, such as cases of layoff or financial difficulties unrelated to candidate performance.

This is one way to protect the recruitment firm from unscrupulous clients who are looking to hire and fire without proper justification.

If the guarantee period is successfully passed and completed, the placement fee is now fully secured with no chance of being clawed back.

In order to minimize the risk of droppers, recruiters strategically build strong relationships and social contracts with both clients and candidates to anticipate any issues that may arise.

They carefully assess everyone's intentions, what's being said/unsaid, and make accurate judgment calls to predict candidate and client behavior.

By adeptly managing both parties, agency recruiters can maintain a high degree of control over the process to ensure that the placement will stick. Experience, vigilance, and a healthy dose of skepticism acts as protection against candidates dropping.

Step 10: Client Pays

Even if the candidate starts, the deal is not over because the last step of the placement process is obtaining payment!

Recruitment firms invoice the client on the day the candidate starts their new role. Clients are contractually obligated to pay within an agreed-upon payment term (could be 7, 10, 14, or 30 days) specified in the contract.

If the client delays payment, it's the recruitment firm's duty to chase the client and their teams to pay the fee to make sure payment timelines are being adhered to.

The guarantee period (industry average of 90 days) is commonly longer than the payment period. The placement process took up so much time that by this point, recruitment firms are eager to be finally rewarded for their services so it's quite common for payment periods to be much shorter than guarantee periods.

In the majority of cases, clients will honor the fee and pay their invoices on time. Even if clients pay late, they usually will pay, albeit needing a little nudge.

Rarely will clients try to weasel out of paying the recruitment fee, provided there are no issues with candidate performance. Even the clients who pay the latest will likely pay out around the time the guarantee period concludes.

There are of course legal repercussions should clients try to skirt recruitment fees as laid out by the contract terms in the recruitment agreement which is why nonpayment is extremely rare.

As with everything in recruitment, nothing is guaranteed! The recruiter is expected to stay on high alert and keep in touch with clients and candidates post placement, ensuring the incoming fee is secure and smoothly processed.

The Deal is Complete!

At this point, the placement is *FINALLY* complete!

In terms of timeline, this entire process may take 2 weeks to 6 months from start to finish, depending on each client and candidate's unique situation which influences the speed of placement.

As always, the agency recruiter is expected to help both parties work together seamlessly to achieve a mutually satisfying outcome.

Overall, recruitment is a dynamic and interesting field to be in, always keeping you on your toes. No two placements are the same! You'll always learn something new from each deal process, whether it closes or not.

Chapter Highlights:

- The agency recruitment deal cycle and process is complicated, lengthy, and fraught with challenges requiring diligence, vigilance, and constant monitoring to progress smoothly.

- The recruitment process consists of 10 steps starting with business development and ending when the candidate passes their guarantee period and the client pays the placement fee.

- Agency recruitment is an exciting career that encompasses a variety of responsibilities beyond just recruiting candidates.

- Recruiters spend much of their time building relationships with, meeting, and entertaining client and candidate networks while leveraging traditional and social media tools on marketing and sales efforts.

- During the recruitment process, many things can go wrong. This is what makes experience and perseverance so important - the more you work in this industry the more you know what to guard against!

- In the worst case outcome of experiencing a dropper, where candidates either quit jobs ahead of their rebate/guarantee period or get fired due to performance, the recruitment firm becomes liable for a full or partial refund or credit to the client, pursuant to the T&Cs.

- The onus is on the agency recruiter to manage every piece of the recruitment process to minimize dropper risk, to ensure clients and candidates are happy with each other, and to continue generating new business in the meantime.

CHAPTER 5

DIRECT HIRE RECRUITMENT

When most people refer to "looking for a job", they're usually speaking of seeking a permanent position. In other words, they want to be directly hired by a company as a W-2 worker.

Due to the lack of universal health insurance in the US, personal preference, career growth, and/or stability reasons, many people aim to be hired on a full-time basis with the associated employee benefits.

This type of recruitment is termed direct hire, synonymous with permanent placement, meaning the employer is looking to hire someone as an internal employee.

Direct Hire Terminology

Agency recruiters who work on direct hire placements are commonly referred to as *Headhunters*.

According to Google, here is the formal definition of "Headhunter":

head·hunt·er
/ˈhedˌ(h)ən(t)ər/
noun

A person who identifies and approaches suitable candidates employed elsewhere to fill business positions.

> *"A headhunter offering you a wonderful new position at a higher salary..."*

This is the most popular and common term direct hire agency recruiters use in order to immediately distinguish themselves from being conflated with an internal recruiter.

"Headhunter" describes agency recruiters well because the job centers around the concept of hunting, *not gathering*. Along the same vein, headhunters proactively target, "hunt", and poach top talent out of their existing roles.

The "head" part of "headhunter" is also apt since headhunters fulfill "headcount" needs as well as work to fill roles for "heads" of departments. The term works beautifully!

The profession of headhunter is a badge of honor because it's a tough, prestigious, high-paying, and overall an aspirational job.

This is why I personally like to use the term "headhunter" when describing my job to the general public. It clearly invokes what this job is about with a sexy spin on it that is meant to sound aggressive, unique, and interesting, a clear differentiator from other terms commonly confused with HR and internal recruitment.

In the USA, "agency recruitment" is primarily used as the most common way to refer to our overarching profession and business as it encompasses both direct hire *and* temp staffing whereas typically "headhunter" *only* refers to direct hire agency recruiters.

Due to the wide range of terms people use to speak about agency recruitment, here are more terms to be aware of:

Executive Search Professional/Recruiter

Recruitment firms that market themselves as specifically targeting executive-level and/or senior-level hires are called executive search firms ("exec search" more casually).

> ① Since headhunters operate globally, this is a widely accepted term. In China, where there is a rapidly growing headhunting industry, you'll commonly hear the phrase 猎头 (liè tóu), meaning "Hunt" (猎) and "Head" (头), the literal translation of headhunter.
>
> In Spanish, headhunters are referred to as cazatalentos, with the word "caza-" meaning hunt and "-talentos" meaning talent.
>
> In the UK and Europe, "headhunter" is also the predominant nomenclature used to describe direct hire/permanent recruitment.
>
> "Headhunter" is a commonly accepted term with no ambiguity in many international markets.
>
> Interestingly enough, in the USA, a small portion of agency recruiters loathe this term and are reluctant to call themselves headhunters. They may associate "headhunter" with sales, something they find distasteful despite this career being clearly and factually a sales career.
>
> This could originate from their personal sense of shame and cultural disdain towards sales and salespeople, wanting to distance themselves from it, which is clearly hypocritical, illusory, and self-deluding.
>
> Thus, despite some people's biases, "headhunter" as a professional term is gaining ground in America, with increasing mass market appeal, recognition, and acceptance.

Due to the fragmentation of this market's terminology and language being less standardized, every company has a *different* definition of what constitutes an executive-level search.

For instance, some firms specifically place true high profile C-suite professionals in Fortune 500 companies, while other firms are tasked to find manager-level staff at a small startup. *Both* may refer to their searches as an executive-level search and they'd both consider themselves to be right.

Any headhunter may classify themselves as an executive search professional or executive search recruiter. They use these terms interchangeably when speaking to customers and the general public.

Commercially, it has a prestigious ring to it, so many recruitment professionals enjoy referring to themselves as such even if they're not recruiting executives by the market's definition or that of their competitors.

Search or Recruitment Professional

"Search" is another industry term that can mean a variety of things. Since there is a huge business in recruiting specifically executives, headhunters may also call themselves "search" professionals referring to executive search in an abbreviated form.

Or it could be referring specifically to the "search" part of the recruitment life cycle, aka the candidate portion.

In the context of "recruitment professional", "recruitment" is shorthand for "agency recruitment". This usually means the recruiter works at some sort of recruitment agency.

Recruiter

While the term "recruiter" is most commonly assumed automatically to mean internal recruiter to most of the general public, many agency recruiters will also refer to themselves as "recruiter".

For ease of speed and because the general public doesn't know the difference anyways, headhunters use this layman's term to convey information quickly without getting sucked into having to explain the nuances and intricacies of internal versus external/agency recruitment.

Since most of the general public doesn't know what the word "headhunter" means, many agency recruiters will simply refer to themselves as "recruiters" for simplicity's sake, so always keep the context in mind when faced with this term to know which type of recruiter is being discussed.

Split-desk v Full-desk

Split-desk v Full-desk is a descriptor term that further provides details on agency recruitment professionals' duties.

A split-desk agency recruiter is "splitting" the desk in half as in, exclusively focused on either the recruitment side or the sales side of the desk. A split-desk recruiter is responsible for delivering candidates to the search, primarily focused on recruitment while a split-desk sales leader is mainly focusing on business development and client/account management.

In contrast, a full-desk* recruitment professional is someone who is tasked with doing *both* ends of the deal (double-ending deals), responsible for recruiting as well as soliciting clients to procure reqs.

*This is not to be confused with the term "full-cycle recruitment", which describes all the responsibilities on specifically the *recruitment* side. Full-desk recruiters are responsible for both full-cycle recruitment in addition to carrying out sales/business development tasks while full-cycle recruiters only deliver on the recruitment end of things.

180°, 270°, and 360° Recruitment Professionals

Since agency recruitment professionals are responsible for different duties depending on which firm they work at and how they're set up, many recruitment agencies (especially UK firms) prefer to describe role duties using the geometric concept of degrees, like in a circle.

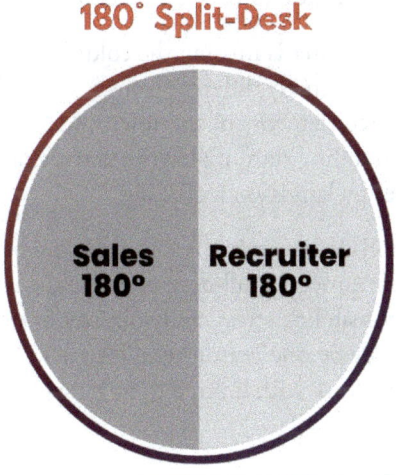

Similar to the term split-desk, a 180° recruiter could be responsible for either sales (180° sales leader/business developer) or recruitment (180° recruiter).

Further along this concept, a 270° recruiter is someone who does recruiting but additionally contributes to managing existing client accounts.

270° Recruiter

A 270° recruiter has more advanced skills working with clients than a 180° recruiter, but they're missing the critical piece of cold-calling and business developing new accounts from scratch.

Since the 270° recruiter is missing the cold-desk buildout sales experience, they're distinctly different from a 360° full-desk recruiter who does all three elements of the role full circle: developing accounts from a standing start, managing said clients, and filling the roles themselves by hands-on recruiting.

Lastly, a 360° full-desk recruiter is someone who has to manage the entire placement process. Full-desk is by far the most challenging role as the responsibility, stress, and consistency needed to build a successful practice by one person requires a lot of attention, dedication, and hard work with limited to no support from other team members.

360°Full Desk Recruiter

For this reason, the career reward, learning pace, financial earning potential, and opportunity is potentially more attractive if one is able to truly fulfill this type of role.

External Recruiter

Unlike internal recruiters, agency recruiters sometimes may use the term "external recruiter" to define what they do as they're a 3rd party, external recruitment partner.

In the past, this used to be a more popular term, but nowadays most people use "agency recruiter" or "headhunter".

Talent Acquisition (TA) or Talent Professional

Many internal recruiters describe themselves as TA professionals.

The TA moniker is confusing because internal recruiters usually call themselves some variation of this, like TA professional, TA manager, TA associate, Head of TA, etc. This makes sense because the HR and recruiting team are internally trying to acquire talent for their teams.

Some agency recruiters lump themselves in with TA in order to draw the attention of candidates and/or brand themselves intentionally as such.

Some willfully use this terminology because they're intentionally trying to pivot out of a recruitment agency and go internal (acquire an internal recruitment job).

While technically it's incorrect as TA refers primarily to internal recruitment duties, there is no set rule stopping agency recruiters from marketing themselves as TA professionals, thus they use the term frequently, albeit incorrectly from the perspective of definition accuracy.

As a general rule of thumb, when it comes to recruitment terminology, avoid making assumptions on what words mean as everyone has their own interpretation and usage of these various terms that may or may not be technically correct.

How Direct Hire Placement Fees Work

This is where the business gets very exciting!

Without further ado, here is the simple rundown of how direct hire placement fees are calculated:

Direct Hire Fee Calculation

Candidate Compensation* ✕ **Fee Percentage*** = **Recruitment Fee/Billings**

***All adhere to contract clauses as previously negotiated & agreed to.**

During the contract negotiation process with clients, two numbers need to be established: the candidate's compensation that the recruiting agency can bill on, and the headhunter's fee percentage.

To calculate the fee, simply multiply the two.

For example, if you signed a client's contract at 20% on a candidate salary offered of $100,000, you would bill the client $20,000.

Similarly, if you place a candidate at a 25% negotiated fee on a $200,000 salary, you would bill the client $50,000.

> ① *Although these numbers are exciting, most recruiters work for a recruitment agency so they do not take the total fee home as personal income!*
>
> *Instead, agency recruiters earn a commission calculated off of the fees they generate. Chapter 8 is entirely dedicated to commission models so you can fully understand how the financial reward trickles down to the producer for those who are employed at recruitment agencies (the majority of recruiters).*
>
> *If an agency recruiter owns their own agency, of course, they would earn the full fee but also be liable for the full costs of running their recruitment business.*

Keep in mind, the candidate's compensation package can constitute many elements and needs to be clarified in the recruitment contract for each client as every contract differs!

While the candidate compensation commonly consists of the base salary only, some savvy recruitment firms have negotiated the percentage to be calculated off of ALL components of the compensation package. This could include sign-on bonuses, future bonuses, car bonuses, home office reimbursements, stock grants/options/units, relocation support, and any other perks.

It's also not unheard of for recruitment contracts to be structured in such a way to receive an additional recruitment fee from the client off of the candidate's second year compensation! Where appropriate, some recruitment firms have negotiated multi-year fee structures where they can continue to earn a residual off of future bonuses/compensation.

When a significant portion of the candidate's income is earned in the future (like in high-end finance sales jobs for instance), this type of fee structure is acceptable and reasonable.

Some startups have also awarded recruitment firms stocks or equity shares as part of or in lieu of the placement fee but that's much less common. After all, recruitment firms are largely risk-averse and financially conservative, preferring to be paid securely in the present rather than receive *potential* payouts in the future.

Commonly, headhunters are trained to negotiate for the most attractive terms as a starting point as best sales practice often dictates. If you can't get everything, at least the hope is that you'll get *something* by being a tough and smart negotiator.

Although some clients and recruiting firms can be flexible to structure their contracts unconventionally, most recruitment contracts keep things simple: for the most part, the fee percentage is charged on the base salary of the placed candidate.

Headhunter Fee Percentages

The recruitment fee is most often a percentage because it is industry standard to do so. Overwhelmingly, the majority of recruitment fee contracts revolve around negotiating a fee percentage to multiply the candidate's compensation by.

In some rare cases, a recruitment firm may charge a flat placement fee but that is an exception to the rule, uncommon to how the majority of traditional recruitment agencies operated in the past and continue to abide by in the present.

Mathematically, a percentage-based fee structure is more advantageous to the recruitment firm so the industry norm is as such. This helps to account for inflation and reward headhunters who place higher value talent as opposed to flat fee structures which don't provide any additional financial reward.

As headhunters' skills rise and their list of clients grow, it's also not uncommon to see headhunters increase their fee percentages because they've curated strong networks and have demonstrated a track record of effectiveness, increasing the value of their services. In the US market, fees tend to be in the 20%-35% range with most agencies working at 20%-25% rates.

While 35% would be an amazing fee percentage to charge and earn consistently, it is quite rare to achieve such a high rate. Many clients, especially if they're desirable accounts, can get away with the mid-to-lower end of fee percentages (20%-25%) since headhunters want to be their vendor and are willing to represent them for a reduced percentage.

Very rarely would US-based recruitment firms accept fee structures of less than 20%. A 10%-15% fee percentage is considered substandard and abysmally low. Most recruitment agencies explicitly prohibit contracts from being signed at under 20% rates due to how much it would decrease profitability.

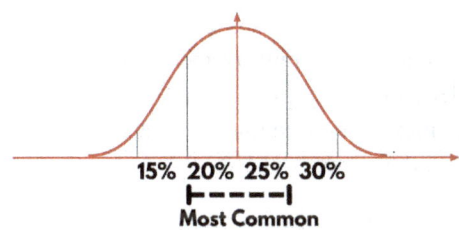

*Rate percentages vary dependent upon market, country, industry, etc.

Reiterating one of Chapter 2's key points, recruitment agencies are selective when it comes to deciding who to service on the client side so they usually forgo partnerships with clients who aren't willing to pay market rate fees.

One factor that can influence headhunter fee percentages is the difficulty of the search. For certain searches and clients, headhunters may charge higher fees knowing that few of their competitors would want to spend their time servicing the search or the client.

Complicating factors that may increase recruitment fees could include: certain hard-to-find skill sets, stringent qualifications to meet, issues facing the management team/organization, office locations that are undesirable/sparsely populated, difficult attitude/outsized expectations of the client, substandard compensation packages offered, and/or lowly regarded market reputation.

Any of these additional risks could reduce or eliminate candidate interest. Therefore, headhunters always have to think strategically before formally partnering with clients, especially those they haven't serviced before.

As headhunters start becoming more successful, they can start charging more for their services, knowing the market so well that they have quite the competitive advantage over other vendors.

People who do *good* business tend to do *well* in business, causing this virtuous cycle to repeat itself as clients and candidates prefer to partner with a recruiter they respect, like, and trust to be top in class.

As much as there are certain averages and commonly accepted pricing models, since this professional service is offered by competing companies in the free market, there is no set rule on what and how to charge clients.

One recruitment firm could offer 10% or a flat-rate fee per hire in order to attract new clients. Another won't charge anything under 30%-35% for the same search. Everyone can dictate their own rates of what they're willing to operate at and how to justify their fee.

> ① *Market to market, industry to industry, region to region, rates and fees differ!* As mentioned, in the UK where the market is very saturated and recruiters must compete on price, their fees can be as low as 10%-15%.
>
> In Asian markets and other developing markets where recruitment is an extremely nascent market that is under-serviced by headhunters, fees can be at 25%-35% on average, stretching to 40%-45% for extremely hard-to-fill searches.

After each successful placement, the client pays the recruitment fee directly to the recruiting firm. The candidate is then internally onboarded by their new employer and will receive all benefits, paychecks, and perks directly from them.

Direct Hire Payment Structure

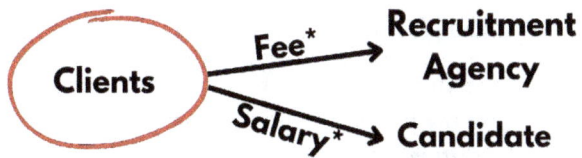

*All adhere to contract clauses as previously negotiated & agreed to.

Candidates and Headhunters Work Together

A important fact to note during the recruitment process is this:

How the client pays the recruitment company and how the client pays the candidate being hired has *nothing* to do with each other.

Some candidates may have the misconception that the recruitment fee is coming out of their pocket or somehow robbing them of salary increases when that couldn't be further from the truth!

In fact, the services candidates receive from agency recruiters are completely *free*.

Firstly, headhunter fees are paid by clients. Plus, candidates receive valuable benefits, including career coaching, direct representation to the headhunter's clients, and full support throughout the process.

Secondly, since the fee percentage is calculated off of the candidate's compensation package, headhunters fight to obtain higher offers for the candidate to earn higher recruitment fees!

Thirdly, headhunters have intimate knowledge of industry-wide compensation data, so they have the ability to inform candidates whether or not they're being underpaid. They can leverage this information to push clients to offer higher rates in order to pay more appropriately.

Ironically, if candidates represent themselves directly to employers without headhunter support, they may end up with *lower* offers due to lack of negotiation support they'd receive from headhunters who are pros at it.

Even more concerningly, internal recruiters' loyalty is to their employer, thus they're more apt to offer candidates *less* in order to decrease hiring and labor costs.

Unlike internal recruiters who only have one opportunity to offer, headhunters have the power to represent top candidates to *multiple* companies, creating bidding wars and strengthening the candidate's hand to negotiate higher offers.

This is why candidates are beneficiaries (not victims!) of headhunters' services. It is a win-win for headhunters and candidates to work together seamlessly and transparently.

Contingent Versus Retained Search

The majority of headhunters work on a contingent basis which means they only earn the fee if the placement is successful.

As discussed in Chapter 4, if the placement fails, the recruitment firm may have to issue a partial or full refund or credit to the client.

To avoid the worst case scenario of losing out on the full fee, an alternative to the contingent model is retained.

On retained searches, headhunters charge the client a non-refundable portion of the fee upfront to initiate the search.

This model is utilized as a way to test and secure a client's partnership through a financial commitment. Furthermore, retained fees ensure that the client is unlikely to use other recruitment agencies to fill the req, decreasing competitive threats.

Other professional service providers, namely attorneys, also work off of retainers so it's not a foreign concept. A retained setup is a common structure that agency recruiters will often pitch clients to consider.

If the client agrees to pay a retained fee upfront, a retainer agreement would have to be negotiated, signed off, and processed.

What is typical in a retained search is that the client will pay a portion of the recruitment fee upfront (usually a third or a half), with the remainder due when the search is completed.

Similar to contingent searches, during the contract negotiation process, a recruitment fee percentage would need to be determined.

However, instead of billing off of the final offer numbers as the search hasn't even begun yet, the fee would be calculated off of a *projected* compensation amount.

Here is the calculation for the 1st part of the retainer fee:

1st Part Retainer Calculation

Projected Candidate Compensation* ✕ **Fee Percentage*** ✕ **Percentage Upfront Due***

*****All adhere to contract clauses as previously negotiated & agreed to.**

In a 2-part retainer structure, 50% of the projected recruitment fee is paid upfront to initiate the search.

If a role has a projected salary of $100,000 and the fee percentage is 25%, then the 1st retained fee charged to the client would be calculated as follows:

$100,000 × 25% × 50% = $12,500

In a 2-part retainer structure, the retained fee to kick off the search would cost the client $12,500.

In a 3-part retainer structure, the retainer consists of 2 fees to be paid in relatively short order:

The first fee kicks off the search and the second fee is due either at the presentation of the official shortlist of candidates (a list of candidates committed to moving to interview) or at the start of interviews.

In a 3-part retainer structure, the first and second fee are the same amount, both 33% of the projected placement fee. Thus, each fee due would be calculated as follows:

$100,000 × 25% × 33% = $8,250

As typical with all recruitment contracts, there are always variations on contract terms depending on what was previously negotiated.

Some contracts calculate 3-part retainers into 3 tranches of payment with more even numbers–30% of the fee due upfront, 30% at the second stage, and the rest of the fee is due when the candidate starts.

For both 2-part and 3-part retainer setups, the remaining portion of the recruitment fee will be invoiced on the day the candidate starts and paid out according to the negotiated payment terms.

To calculate the final retained fee due, begin by multiplying the actual candidate compensation (the offer accepted by the candidate) by the recruitment fee percentage.

Next, deduct all the retained fees the client has already paid, leaving the final amount to be invoiced to the client on the candidate's start date.

The final retainer fee due could be a lot higher or lower than expected due to the candidate's actual compensation number varying greatly from initial projections.

Final Portion Retainer Calculation

ACTUAL Candidate Compensation* ✕ **Fee Percentage*** = **Previously Paid out Retainer Amount(s)**

*All adhere to contract clauses as previously negotiated & agreed to.

To illustrate this, let's say the final compensation number ended up being $120,000 because the client chose a more senior candidate who needed a higher offer amount to accept the role.

In a 2-part retained structure, the final portion of the recruitment fee due would be calculated as follows:

$120,000 × 25% − $12,500 = $17,500

In a 3-part retained structure, the final portion of the recruitment fee due would be calculated as follows:

$120,000 × 25% − ($8,250 + $8,250) = $13,500

Conversely, if a great candidate is found with slightly less experience or lower compensation requirements, their offer may be less than the target salary, resulting in a lower final retainer fee due.

To illustrate this, let's say the final compensation number ended up being $80,000.

In a 2-part retained structure, the final portion of the recruitment fee due would be calculated as follows:

$80,000 × 25% − $12,500 = $7,500

In a 3-part retained structure, the final portion of the recruitment fee due would be calculated as follows:

$80,000 × 25% − ($8,250 + $8,250) = $3,500

In both 2- and 3-part retainer setups, the total fee paid out doesn't change but there is one key difference from a contingent placement:

The pre-paid retained portions of the fee are typically non-refundable.

If the candidate doesn't work out, the only part of the fee exposed to potential dropper risk is the last and final portion of the retainer fee.

This is the advantage of a retained search setup and why many agency recruiters prefer to work retained–they get to keep at least half to two-thirds of the projected recruitment fee *regardless* if the candidate works out or not.

Engaged/Contained Searches

In recent years, some recruitment firms have started to offer clients an enticing low flat rate initial engagement fee or low recurring fees in an effort to land new clients.

Many agency recruiters call this an "engaged" or "contained" search, hoping to secure an exclusive recruitment partnership by offering a much cheaper initial and/or ongoing fee compared to the more expensive retainer option.

As much as some select recruitment professionals and firms like to offer this structure in more recent years, this is not the standard pricing practice at most recruitment firms because there is a hidden downside risk to accepting what is essentially, a small cash advance.

As an insider, I actually find these strategies to be extremely dangerous; it could actually backfire on the recruiter who is entangled by this setup for this key reason:

Recruitment contracts usually offer non-solicitation clauses that preclude recruitment firms from poaching from the client, for an industry standard of 12 months from the moment any payment is received.

In a contingent search, since no fees are paid upfront, a recruitment firm has the freedom to turn on a client should things go awry and the partnership ends.

However, once any amount of money is paid out to the recruitment firm, the client has a stronger legal right to argue that the recruitment firm is now a paid agent and partner, thus must respect non-solicitation clauses.

This loophole allows insincere clients to take advantage of recruitment firms by paying a low container fee to hold the recruitment firm back from poaching their staff, *without the true intention of ever hiring!*

In markets with a very limited number of candidates available, signing away poaching rights for a low one-time or recurring payment could be financially detrimental to the recruiter's business, should the client be revealed to be operating under bad faith.

To make matters worse, clients feel psychologically entitled to recruiters' services, attention, and time the minute they pay an invoice, no matter how small!

Even if the engagement fee is a mere $3,000-$5,000, clients may start imposing demands on recruitment firms the same way as if they were under a proper retained search agreement.

Clients being clients, may become dissatisfied, angry, or upset if they feel they're not receiving the value they expected from the recruitment firm or if the firm fails to fulfill their end of the bargain.

In such cases, it raises the question: Was the low engagement fee worth the ensuing hassle and drama?

All that being said, as with everything in the world of recruitment, there's no one-size-fits-all approach! Some recruiters may only work on retained while others prefer contingent or contained.

Nowadays, many firms offer an array of structures for clients to choose from in order to remain flexible and creative, presenting multiple search and pricing options to win clients over.

Ultimately, each recruitment firm has to determine their own market strategy in order to adapt quickly and thrive within the competitive landscape of their niche.

> **Chapter Highlights:**
>
> - Direct hire recruitment solves clients' hiring needs for full-time staff. The recruitment firm finds candidate(s) for the client to interview and if the candidate accepts the offer and starts their new role, the recruitment firm receives a fee calculated as a percentage of the candidate's compensation package.
>
> - Recruitment firms can charge an upfront retainer fee, meaning the client pays a negotiated non-refundable portion of the fee before the recruiter starts delivering on the open req.
>
> - If the client and recruitment firm are working together on a contingent basis, the fee is paid out in full after the candidate starts their role.
>
> - Retained searches are commonly offered in a 2-part or 3-part structure.
>
> - Some firms also charge on a "contained" or "engaged" basis.
>
> - Recruitment companies can be creative in their pricing and contract terms and it varies per industry, country, and market. No two contracts are guaranteed to be the same.

CHAPTER 6

STAFFING

Besides providing direct hire placement services, recruitment agencies play a critical role to help clients find, secure, and hire temporary staff. This market is just as big as perm recruitment, if not, *bigger*.

Businesses frequently need extra labor support and temporary staff to deliver on time-bound projects. As much as the internal team already exists, sometimes they don't have the right people on staff or *enough* staff.

The company may not be in a position to hire more full-time staff in time to achieve business objectives due to how long the recruitment process takes. This is where staffing agencies enter the picture!

Staffing Terminology

Recruitment firms who focus on staffing, staffing agencies, could also be called contract recruitment businesses, interim staffing, contract recruiting, staff augmentation services, temp/temporary staffing, securing consultants, contractor placement, etc.

Clients need to hire temporary workers (temps) also known as contractors, consultants, and freelancers, to work on a contractual basis for a set time period as a short-term solution instead of committing to hiring more people on full-time.

Since staffing is a bit more complicated than direct hire, it's actually easier for staffing teams to deliver on contract and supplement direct hiring needs than the reverse.

Headhunters and staffing professionals operate very differently because temp and perm candidate pools have completely different mindsets, approaches, motivations, career trajectories, and preferences.

This is why most recruitment agencies and recruiters specialize and usually are stronger at placing one or the other.

Due to the confusing and fragmented nature of the recruitment industry, every firm uses different terminology, but "staffing" is commonly accepted as an appropriate term to describe temp/contract recruitment businesses.

> ① *You may encounter terms like RPO (Recruitment Process Outsourcing or Recruitment Professional Offsite/Outsourced) or MSP (Managed Service Provider). These are different services and business models providing outsourced services for talent management, recruitment, and HR functions, not to be confused with traditional recruitment agency services.*
>
> *There is some limited interaction between recruitment firms who are forced to collaborate with MSPs for certain clients who choose to utilize these 3rd party talent augmentation services.*
>
> *Some clients will utilize a mix of RPOs, MSPs, and recruitment firms, as they need different solutions for different divisions, roles, functions, and types of talent within their organization.*
>
> *Companies may outsource all or much of their talent management and recruitment needs to 3rd parties due to financial and business reasons. RPO firms function more like outsourced internal recruiters that are assigned to serve solely one client, which is completely different from traditional recruitment agency setups.*
>
> *Thus, for the purposes of AR101, I will not cover RPOs or MSPs as they do not function the same as traditional recruitment firms structurally, financially, and operationally.*

Staffing works similarly to direct hire recruitment, although it's much more common for staffing teams to be set up in a split desk model.

A 180° salesperson handles the client side, bringing in new accounts and managing existing accounts, while the recruiting team, also known as the delivery team, procures, submits, and manages candidates from identification and initial outreach to post placement contractor care.

A client-side staffing professional is commonly referred to as: account executive (AE), account manager (AM), client development specialist, client manager, business development manager, sales lead, etc.

While some firms may use the terms Account Managers and Business Developers interchangeably, there is a notable difference in the skillset of *new* business development professionals versus those who just manage *existing* accounts.

True business developers who have the skills to bring in *new* clients are rewarded differently as hunters than those who only manage *existing* accounts as farmers.

A 180° recruiter working on the delivery team is commonly referred to as: delivery specialist, recruiter, staffing specialist, contract recruiter, sourcer, etc.

As discussed in Chapter 9, there are levels of seniority and career progression on both sides of the desk so directors of delivery/recruitment as well as sales directors exist.

The reason why staffing tends to operate more on a split-desk model compared to direct hire where many agency recruiters operate a full-desk is because the volume and urgency of temp hiring needs is typically much higher.

On a project, instead of just hiring one person, multiple contractors may be needed. The turnaround time for the job order is much quicker as well (e.g. the client may need two contractors to start the next week).

Thus, this division of labor allows recruiters and sales leaders to build robust networks quickly on their side of the desk, leading to economies of scale and faster time-to-fill rates.

Temp to Perm Conversions

Often, candidates who start off working within a contracting capacity eventually shift into a full-time role, also known as converting from temp to perm. Another term for this is "contract to hire".

Perhaps, a client wants to bring someone on full-time eventually but would prefer to test them out on the job first. It's also quite possible that a client and candidate enjoy working together so much that a full-time offer is extended to the contractor in an effort to retain them for the long haul.

In either case, they start off by hiring a contractor first to evaluate their performance on the job, work ethic, and cultural fit.

It's often sold as a "try before you buy" solution for clients if they are unsure about a candidate or don't have a budget allocated for a full-time hire at that precise moment. This is an attractive option in the meantime for clients to make a hire regardless.

Like in a typical contractor arrangement, recruitment agencies get paid for every hour worked by the contractor but also can charge a "conversion fee" if and when the client "converts" the candidate to a full-time employee.

This fee is a reasonable ask because once the contractor is converted into a permanent hire, the recruitment firm can no longer profit from each hour the contractor works! In order to offset the loss of future income, the recruitment firm charges this "conversion fee".

While it's not financially ideal to lose a contractor to a one-time conversion fee (a smaller amount compared to if the candidate remained a contractor), recruitment firms will do so in order to keep their clients and candidates happy.

At the end of the day, the recruitment firm is delicately balancing profit maximization while servicing their clientele satisfactorily.

Therefore, it's always important to remain nimble, flexible, and open-minded to strive for win-win scenarios over short term profit for the health of the long-term partnership.

Keep in mind, while some contractors may end up converting into permanent hires if there is a mutual desire to do so, most professional contractors staunchly enjoy their lifestyle as a contractor and would never consider switching to perm. Their reasons are illuminating as we'll explore further in the next section.

Why Contracting is Attractive

Before I knew anything about the agency recruitment business, I always assumed that the only definition of "having a job" is being a full-time employee. I didn't understand why people would be open to, much less *prefer*, working a contract or freelance role.

From an employer's perspective, I thought, "Why would companies want to hire someone on an hourly basis when they have the option of hiring someone full-time? What's in it for them to hire temp workers instead of getting more value, consistency, and loyalty from an internal direct hire?"

Similarly, from the employee's vantage point, I wondered, "Why would anyone forgo a full-time job and instead prefer a fixed term contract? Don't they care about healthcare benefits and PTO?"

Well, as with everything in recruitment and employment, there is diversity in working setups! For some people and companies, there are strong justifications why a contractor setup can be more attractive than full-time employment.

Perhaps, a company may be going through a time of transition, have serious work overflows, or is experiencing a merger/acquisition that requires a lot of temporary help.

Or, they could've had a critical person leave or go on a break. Until they find the perfect replacement or that person comes back, they can't afford to have the work go unattended. In this case, going straight for a permanent hire, a time-consuming process, may not be a suitable solution because they needed someone in the seat *yesterday*.

Bringing on a contractor gives the team time to hire for the perfect perm candidate while the work is still being covered in the meantime. Furthermore, employers are not liable to pay for benefits, PTO, equity (options, stock grants), and/or other perks for temp staff, saving a pretty penny!

Here are some examples of clients hiring contractors to fulfill short term project needs:

- If a pharmaceutical company is submitting a big FDA (Food & Drug Administration) filing for a NDA (new drug application), they will hire multiple contractors to pitch in. Because the filing presents short-term pressure that requires more staff, and they don't know whether or not the drug will be approved, it makes sense to bring people on an interim basis to support the intensity of the drug approval process.

- When an accounting firm needs more accountants to support clients during the tax busy season, they turn to temp recruiters specializing in placing accountants to help with work overflow.

- If a legal firm has a sudden influx of client work that needs supplemental legal review specialists but the increased workload is only a temporary phenomenon, they will engage a recruitment agency that specifically provides temp workers for the legal field.

- If a bank is facing an audit from the SEC (Securities and Exchange Commission), which is hopefully a temporary situation, they would prefer to hire short-term help, instead of committing to the hefty costs of adding internal staff.

- Then, there are life circumstances that pop up, aka someone is out on parental leave, thus they need a contractor to help out in the interim.

> ⓘ *In a way, staffing firms are competing directly against consulting firms that profit off of projects by hiring full-time consultants then subcontracting them out to various projects. Recruitment firms, similarly, go up for bids through a process called RFPs (Request For Proposals) in order to obtain projects to work on, called SOWs (Statement of Work).*
>
> *SOWs are the holy grail because it basically guarantees that the firm has won the bid, therefore securing profits for the duration of the approved project.*
>
> *Interestingly enough, traditional consulting firms compete with staffing firms to win SOWs to provide project support and staff augmentation services. In recent years, some recruitment firms have gained ground and market share in certain niches.*
>
> *While consulting and recruitment businesses are similar, they're not the same by definition, classification, and operation. Thus, in AR101, I won't cover consulting because it falls outside the scope of traditional agency recruitment.*

As explained, not only do clients prefer the temp setup, there is a fair portion of professionals who exclusively prefer to work as contractors as well!

They own their own business and enjoy their freelance status due to the freedom of not needing to work a job in the traditional sense. Furthermore, contractors in certain markets and specialisms can earn a high hourly wage, sometimes double to quadruple what their permanent counterparts make!

This is partly due to companies not needing to pay their benefits or any other perks. The business budget is then capable of affording high contractor fees for short-term engagements. Furthermore, since contractors can shop their abilities out to multiple employers, they can command a high hourly rate due to the competitive landscape.

In niche markets where there is an extremely limited supply of temp specialists available, this is *especially* the case. The hourly rate specialists command in markets where very few people are qualified is eye-poppingly high.

However, contractors' work opportunities aren't guaranteed as firms can end contracts on a moment's notice due to a decrease in demand for their services, performance issues, budget constraints, etc.

Every labor market works differently. In some markets, full-time workers all-in earn more than their contract counterparts with salary, bonuses, equity, and benefits, while the opposite is also true where contractors outearn perm workers by significant margins.

Due to how limited the number of people are in certain specialized fields, it's quite possible that contractors can charge quite a premium for projects, freeing them up to work less overall while making more money. Or, they're not motivated to hold down a job, dislike office politics, and simply enjoy contracting. These are all valid reasons for why some people may prefer contracting.

Contractors can also influence their pay rate. If they're more qualified, better at selling themselves, and can manage their business overheads well, they can further increase their hourly pay rate and profit margins.

Contractors essentially run their own business and are entrepreneurs in their own right. On the bright side, they can allocate abundant time for breaks between projects while avoiding workplace politics full-time hires have to deal with.

However, as with all business owners, their responsibilities are higher. They must obtain their own healthcare, manage business operating costs, and maintain all the tools they need to run their own day-to-day activities.

This is why many contractors are married to spouses with full-time employment, accessing corporate and health benefits that cover the entire family unit while the spouse who works as a contractor earns a higher hourly wage providing more flexibility.

For all of these reasons, providing staffing services is a wide reaching and ubiquitous commercial opportunity that agencies cash in on *big time*!

The Critical Role Staffing Agencies Play

Now that you understand what staffing is, what role do staffing agencies play?

In other words, why do staffing agencies exist if contractors and clients can work together directly on their projects?

The easiest way to explain this is examining the similar pain points and work experiences temp *and* full-time staff have which boils down to this:

Like their perm counterparts, contractors are too busy working, making a living, managing their personal life, etc., that they do not have the time nor want to find their next work assignment on their own!

Because staffing professionals service the market 24/7, they have a wealth of knowledge about current hiring trends, hourly rates, which employers are desirable, firms' culture, and which firms pay well.

Not only that, the staffing agency actually vets the merit of the project too. Partnering with a staffing firm takes a lot of the guesswork out of whether or not the project will be confirmed in addition to providing QC (quality control) on the legitimacy of the project and client.

These are some of the reasons why it's easier for contractors to find work through this simplified process utilizing the support and expertise of staffing firms instead of DIYing the whole process.

Additionally, there are administrative, financial, and legal benefits as many of these staffing firms provide payrolling services to the contractors who choose to utilize them, decreasing their administrative burden on invoicing and other back office tasks.

If they decide to work directly with a client without the assistance of a staffing firm, they will have to personally shoulder these responsibilities and the associated costs. They'd also have to go through the trouble of invoicing clients and collecting payment themselves.

If clients pay later than desired (which is not uncommon), the contractor might not have cash flow for a period of time. Not only that, if the client continues to delay payment, the contractor has to go through the effort of collections which is an unpleasant task in addition to being costly and time consuming.

When working through a staffing firm, these risks are eliminated because the staffing firm pays the contractor on a guaranteed timeline that was previously agreed upon, regardless of when the client pays.

Therefore, the staffing firm takes on the risk of non- or late payment while the contractor has assurance of getting paid. This transfers the duty (and risk) of payment collection to the staffing agency, relieving the contractor of this stressful obligation.

Another critical role staffing firms play is ensuring that their contractors are always kept busy! They work as a sales agent on behalf of the contractor to line up gigs for them and pipeline future projects. Since staffing professionals are paid only when the contractor is working through them, they're incentivized to consistently seek out attractive projects that may appeal to their contractor pool.

This combined service offering makes top staffing firms really useful for contractors to leverage repeatedly. The contractors can focus on project tasks and execution, without dealing with the headache of business operations, as the staffing firm takes care of everything for them.

In addition to these tangible benefits, staffing firms serve as a go-between, arbitrator, and negotiator between the contractor and the client. This ongoing communication support helps guide both parties to build a stronger and smoother working relationship.

As great as these benefits are, unlike direct hire recruitment, there is a cost to the contractor utilizing a staffing agency's services, which I'll explain in the next segment.

How Staffing Firms are Paid

From a revenue perspective, the biggest difference between placing contractors versus permanent workers is that direct hire placements are paid in one lump sum versus staffing placements which pay out on a residual and recurring basis for as long as the contractor is working through the staffing firm.

While it's no easy feat, staffing professionals can take home eye-popping numbers just as much as, *if not more than*, direct hire recruiters.

Contract revenue is more complex than direct hire revenue as there are more moving parts. In this chapter, I'll go through how contract revenue is calculated. As to how much the *individual* earns from a commission standpoint, that will be separately addressed in Chapter 8.

To recap, once the client finds the right candidate and makes an offer that is accepted, the staffing firm supports the smooth onboarding and ongoing employ of the contractor.

Unlike in direct hire where the client has to pay the candidate their salary and benefits and the recruitment firm the one-time placement fee separately, in staffing, the client only pays *one* party, the staffing firm.

The staffing agency pays the candidate instead of the client taking on that direct relationship like in a direct hire situation. This is because the business relationship is between the staffing firm the contractor is working through and the client.

As seen in the illustration, there are many additional components in staffing that direct hire simply does not have.

Staffing placements are much more complicated and burdensome from an administrative, legal, financial, and tax perspective than the simple transaction that direct hire placement is.

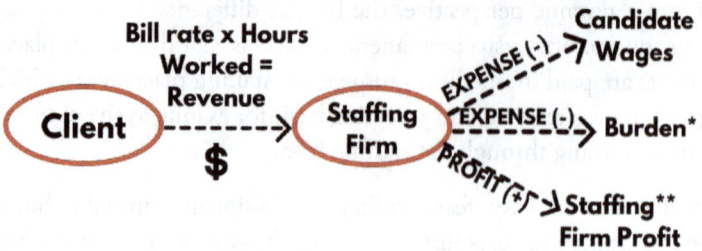

*Burden consists of taxes & other costs, percentages vary
**Other terms: Gross profit, gross margin, spread, net profit

In temp placements, a number of new terms are part of the equation to determine what the staffing firm's profit is after everything is accounted for, which include:

Bill Rate: This is how much the staffing firm charges the client per hour the contractor works. This range is previously discussed and agreed to during the contract negotiation process.

Revenue: This is calculated by multiplying the hours the contractor worked (as evidenced by the time sheets they've updated) by the bill rate. The staffing firm invoices the client for this amount.

The revenue the staffing firm earns then goes on to pay for 2 expenses: the contractor's pay, as well as the "burden".

Burden: This accounts for the administrative, legal, and back office fees that the agency pays each hour the contractor works. It's typically a percentage that the agency sets to encompass all of these expenses, such as worker's compensation insurance, taxes for federal unemployment, state unemployment insurance, social security, Medicare, accounting fees, legal fees, payroll services, administrative support fees, etc.

Since the staffing firm is paying the contractor, they're responsible for withholding federal, state, and/or city taxes thus they charge a burden.

Every firm has different cost structures so the burden percentage varies from firm to firm. Generally, the burden is 20-30% of the bill rate. Of course, this varies by firm, market requirements, and industry peculiarities.

For instance, recruitment firms supporting critical government projects at a high security clearance could potentially require higher burdens. Staffing firms servicing factories/manufacturing facilities, healthcare/medical/clinical centers, and oil rigs would face more risk and liability which would increase burden percentages to account for additional insurance costs.

Pay Rate: This is the amount per hour the contractor is paid. Since contractors can negotiate for their own rates, it's in the contractor's best interest to push up their rate as much as they can. However, there will be limits to how much each recruitment firm can afford to pay.

Recruiting firms must account for the burden as well as what the client's budget is. Therefore, they can only present candidates to the position if the rate works for all 3 parties (staffing firm, client, and candidate).

If a contractor charges too much, then the recruitment firm would not be able to partner with them. Staffing professionals have to diligently negotiate rates to satisfy both the client and candidate while accounting for their own desired profit margins too!

Staffing firm profit: After subtracting the 2 expenses of burden and cost of the candidate's wages from the revenue, you'll end up with the staffing firm's profit for that particular placement.

As long as the contractor continues to work for the client, the staffing firm will continue to collect the associated profit.

Every firm has their own preferred way of measuring and describing profit, otherwise termed as: "spread", "gross margin (GM)", "net profit", or "gross profit (GP)". Usually this term is referred to on a monthly or weekly basis, as in "weekly spread" or "monthly GM".

Essentially, the client ends up paying a premium, aka "markup" on the candidate's hourly wage, which is usually expressed as a percentage.

> ⓘ *Do not conflate revenues with spreads or markups. Revenue is a top line number which only reflects the total amount billed to the client without accounting for the costs associated with doing business.*
>
> *Because every staffing agency has a different cost structure, the revenue number doesn't tell the full story.*
>
> *Instead, gross profit/spread is a much more important number as it is what remains after the contractor's wages and the burden is deducted. More importantly, staffing professionals' commissions are calculated off of the spread they procured, NOT revenue.*

Staffing firms work hard to ensure that the numbers work out in everyone's favor. Yet again, they're trying to achieve a 3-way win scenario.

Thus, it's helpful to set clear and transparent guidelines that are predetermined on what the markup ranges should be in order to remain competitive and reasonable according to market and labor conditions.

Every niche market has different market averages when it comes to markup percentages, ranging from as low as 30% to as high as 100%-300%. It takes experience, commercial/financial common sense, and niche knowledge to figure this out.

In unique situations where qualified contractors are extremely hard to procure, their markup can be on the higher end because clients have no choice but to pay these markups to secure talent.

If there aren't enough recruitment firms servicing the niche, the markups could remain high for quite some time! These extremely attractive market niches are a staffing agency's dream.

The client usually gives a range and the sales leader will negotiate and try to push for flexibility to raise the rate in order to be more attractive to the market so that the employer can find a temp worker faster.

The more an employer is willing to pay, the easier and faster the recruiter can then recruit contractors to join the project.

Another big difference to note between direct hire and staffing is that staffing firms are financially incentivized to negotiate lower candidate pay rates in order to increase the firm's profit margin.

Unlike direct hire where the more the candidate makes, the more the headhunter makes, in staffing, the firm actually loses money if they pay the contractors more than necessary!

As much as contractors may be worried they're getting taken advantage of, this rarely happens in practice, which is why contractors and staffing agencies consistently choose to symbiotically work together.

In reality, competitive market forces and accessible market data like pay rates ensure that underpaid contractors eventually will course correct. Once they find out what they ought to be paid, they may exit contracts that pay too little and re-negotiate rates that are more market-conforming.

Aligned with economic theory, there is an element of the invisible hand concept where the market self-regulates and is constantly re-adjusting to fit the needs of everyone participating in the exchange of goods and services, in this case, labor.

This won't stop staffing firms from charging as high a markup as they can get away with at times, but it regulates the market to be more fair *for the most part*.

The threat of competitors and clients/candidates switching staffing partners keeps everyone honest and willing to be flexible on rates.

Markups are susceptible to labor supply and demand changes, so they're never static and can fluctuate year to year, season to season.

For example, during tax filing time, temp accountants may charge more than they normally would. Staffing firms understand these cyclical factors and will incorporate the impact of seasonality and other market factors into their pricing strategy.

> ① *Recruitment businesses that earn a significant amount of profit from their staffing services are more commercially valued than direct hire heavy recruitment businesses.*
>
> *Since many direct hire headhunters are full-desk and overheads are lower to operate, it's much easier for them to leave their employer and set up an independent practice.*
>
> *In contrast, retention risks associated with staffing firms are lower because staffing businesses require more capital to set up and operate, creating higher barriers to entry.*
>
> *Moreover, top billers in staffing earn more due to the scalability of the split-desk model and ongoing commissions from long-term projects. Staffing sales leaders, if situated well, can build up an impressive contractor book over the years, leading to consistent, residual, and compounding income growth. Thus, it's actually easier and more lucrative for staffing top billers to continue working for their employer, minimizing attrition risk which benefits both employers and investors of recruitment businesses.*
>
> *Companies interested to buy, merge, or invest into recruitment firms highly value income streams beyond the sporadic one-time lump-sum nature of direct hire revenues. Contractors, since they work on projects that go on for many months and potentially 2 years, are a more reliable income source, making staffing businesses a more attractive investment and acquisition target.*
>
> *This is why many recruitment owners and firms want to build out their temp capabilities and staffing offering; they'd like to get a higher multiplier for their firm and juice up their business's value, which is hard to do without a significant book of contractors and staffing clients.*

Over time, markups may decrease in certain markets as competition increases and the space gets more saturated. Staffing firms have to constantly adjust on rates in order to retain clients and contractors.

If the engagement goes well, the client may extend the contract, creating a nice stream of recurring and residual revenue for the firm.

Even more attractive, its effect is amplified the more contractors the staffing firm has out on billing!

Mathematically, since temp contracts may last up to two years per contractor, the total deal value over such a long time frame could greatly outpace direct hire fees. This can become a formidable source of income the bigger the number of contractors is and the longer the contract length becomes.

Firms employing large numbers of contractors usually have robust internal teams that help provide contractor support post placement, while other firms with a small staffing component may outsource some admin and payrolling systems to third party businesses that specifically help recruitment firms manage and process contractors.

In either case, the onus is on the staffing firm to keep in touch with their contractors to ensure satisfaction with their services and clients, which will hopefully result in a continued partnership.

Similar to direct hire, the profits earned by the staffing firm are divvied up internally according to predetermined commission schedules with more on this topic in Chapter 8.

Now that you understand what direct hire and staffing is all about, let's continue onto the more exciting topic of compensation components both types of recruiters will be able to earn!

Chapter Highlights:

- Staffing firms are utilized by clients who need to hire short-term project support and longer term contractor engagements, maxing out at 2 years per client site.

- Some contractors convert into full-time hires in a process called "temp-to-perm" conversion.

- Staffing professionals are able to profit off of each hour any contractor they place works, leading to incredible wealth building opportunities due to the compounding and residual income effects of this setup.

- The split-desk model is common in staffing, where sales and recruiting teams handle different aspects of the process.

- Staffing profits goes by a variety of weekly and monthly terms, most commonly "weekly spread" and "monthly gross margin (GM)".

- Staffing revenues, profits, and markups are different numbers which are calculated differently.

- In extremely niche and emerging markets, staffing firms can reap high profits as the pay rates and contract length for qualified candidates could be so generous that despite heavier administrative, tax, and labor costs, the spread could be phenomenal.

- Staffing professionals must keep in touch with their clients and candidates to ensure projects continue to go well in hopes of expanding existing, repeat, and future business.

- Due to lower retention issues and high profitability, recruitment firms with strong staffing capabilities and contractor books are more valuable than recruitment firms reliant on direct hire in the eyes of investors.

CHAPTER 7

COMPENSATION COMPONENTS

Agency recruitment is a profession where it's hard to find information on how compensation works. This is why AR101 dedicates *two* chapters to this very topic!

In this chapter, we will explore all possible compensation components recruiters can earn, excluding commission. Commission structures are incredibly diverse and complex, deserving a dedicated breakdown on the subject coming up next in Chapter 8.

As an additional complication, because agency recruiting is a sales career, not everyone will earn the same amount of money. In each firm, top billers could be making double to quintuple(!) what their peers make.

While no two recruitment firms have the same exact compensation model, in order to encourage and incentivize staff to perform better, compensation plans are commonly designed to reward those who reach higher production numbers.

Top performers are eligible to access more perks, higher rewards, and exclusive compensation components low- to medium-level performers won't qualify to earn.

Let's break down common compensation components you can expect recruitment firms to offer top performers.

Base Salary or Draw

While some agency recruiters own their own practice, most, especially those starting out, work for a recruitment agency first to "learn and earn on someone else's dime and time".

Under the terms of their employment contract, they are compensated according to their firm's compensation structure, detailed in their offer letter and onboarding materials.

Some recruitment firms offer a salary which is a yearly amount that the company is contractually obligated to pay the employee. Other firms prefer to pay their producers on a draw which functions just like a salary does but there are strings attached with how future commissions are paid out (more on this in Chapter 8).

For the purposes of this section and to keep things simple for now, a draw functions like a base salary in the sense that it is paid out bi-weekly or monthly. For many people, this monthly amount, while not as high as salaries in other fields, nevertheless helps producers get by and offset their cost of living while waiting for commissions to come in.

In terms of US salary ranges, the yearly base or draw for entry-level recruiters could be as low as $35k-$45k nationally. In many metropolitan cities with high costs of living such as New York City, San Francisco, and Los Angeles, the yearly base or draw could be as high as $40k-$60k.

There are two profiles that are exceptions to the rule and can command higher starting salaries due to possessing relevant industry knowledge:

1. Accountants who transition into accounting recruitment can receive offers ranging from $60k-$80k.
2. Lawyers with JDs who recruit other lawyers can receive offers starting at $80k-$100k or more.

These two recruitment markets value industry experience which is reflected in the pay for recruiters with technical knowledge and credentials in these niche fields.

Like all W-2 employees working on a salaried basis, agency recruiters receive common full-time employee benefits like PTO, healthcare, 401k plan, etc.

However, it's important to note that recruitment agencies may not excel in the benefits department compared to other industries that invest in robust perks. This is because recruiters' primary focus and goal is to maximize commission income, resulting in the bulk of recruitment firm spending being allocated to performance-based incentives.

Incentive Trips

Many recruitment firms set up quarterly and/or yearly trips to encourage people to hit their billing targets required to qualify for these expensive outings.

The trips are usually all expenses paid to places like Cabo, Cancun, famous beach towns, or ski destinations like Brekenridge/Tahoe, or wherever else is trending and perceived as high value.

In Europe, clubbing in Ibiza or skiing in Switzerland are common incentives you can expect recruitment firms to tout.

These trips are fun for staff because it gives them something to work toward throughout the year and is a fun way to incentivize people to achieve their targets. As with most sales businesses, recruitment firms leverage incentive trips to drive team and individual performance.

Especially for younger staff that haven't been able to go to luxurious resorts and locales before, the idea of an all-expenses paid trip with other top billers to hot spots around the country and world could be super fun and motivating!

Culturally, it builds camaraderie between disparate teams as top performers can look forward to meeting like-minded and similarly accomplished people at these events to build relationships with their colleagues.

These incentive trips are called something prestigious like president's club, chairman's club, top biller incentive, or superbillers' trip. Top performers who "hit" these trips benefit politically and career-wise. Thus, many ambitious agency recruiters strive to rank among this elite group.

> ① *Some firms even offer free trips by default to the entire company. This is because they may have an annual meeting and/or training events they'd like their staff to attend. Usually, they pay for their staff's travel and lodging, another perk some recruiters experience if they work at a firm offering this type of setup.*

Competitions

Similar to incentive trips, recruitment firms get creative to keep performers motivated on a continual basis. While the yearly and/or quarterly incentive trips can be exciting, they could be too hard for everyone to hit. Thus, short-term, smaller rewards are utilized to inspire people to achieve.

For example, many UK firms may offer a monthly event called "lunch club", a popular incentive that recruiters can qualify for if they bill past a certain amount in a month.

If recruiters achieve this, their reward is to leave work early to eat and drink on the company's dime at the best restaurants in town on the last Friday of the month in which they hit their billing target.

This is a common and effective incentive because there is always buzz in the office of who hit lunch club or not. Due to the monthly pressure and desire for existing and aspiring top billers to hit lunch club as frequently as possible, they create and buy into a culture of urgency, high performance, and high standards.

Another very popular reward at recruitment firms (especially UK ones) is the Rolex incentive. Every year, only a select few of the highest ranking billers will win this coveted prize.

Since Rolexes are a high value status symbol, this could drive performance due to the immense prestige and ultimate bragging right of this incredible honor.

International and national recruitment businesses can get even more creative. Some have offered office swaps, which means if you hit certain billing targets, you may be eligible to earn a free trip to another office to work out of.

On the smallest level of reward, recruitment firms may offer gift cards, event tickets, or spa vouchers for people who hit daily, weekly, or monthly KPI targets or other metrics.

By gamifying the reward system, recruitment firms hope to motivate their staff on a continual basis to do the best they can to exceed their own expectations.

Compensation Increases

The easiest way agencies can incentivize their staff to do more deals is to offer base salary and commission rate increases after recruiters have reached their billing targets and performance markers.

Most firms will clearly lay out promotion targets so that producers know exactly what they need to achieve in order to level up.

As people produce more money for the firm, it gives them the option to open up new divisions, move up internally, and negotiate for raises. For firms with a regional, national, or global presence, it's not uncommon for top billers to be wooed by different teams internally with raises and career advancement opportunities.

At certain points in one's career, it's important to take the initiative and renegotiate what additional compensation and commission increases are available. While some raises are straightforward to achieve, career advancement and/or additional desired compensation needs to be fought for through self-advocacy.

Team Overrides

As recruitment professionals matriculate through the career ladder laid out in Chapter 9, some recruiters decide to take on leadership responsibilities which consist of managing, training, and developing staff.

Managing staff usually comes with some sort of financial reward, called a team override. The override percentage ranges in the low single digits and is multiplied by the team's billings to calculate the override bonus amount. It's also common for team managers to receive a small base increase to take on the duties of training and developing staff.

If your team becomes successful at billing, you, as the team leader, will profit from their production by collecting these override bonuses.

> ① *Not every commission plan is set up for managers to win. Always read the fine print. Due to the high turnover rate of entry-level recruiters, the odds of a future top biller being assigned to you are low.*
>
> *If your team is too junior and/or just not very good, they will not produce revenue consistently and at a high enough level to commission off of profitably. Another potential concern is the high investment of time it takes to train staff up to become self-sufficient, decreasing the ROI on time spent managing.*

For managers leading teams that are achieving or exceeding their billing targets, management could be rewarding both personally as well as financially.

For teams that don't perform well, the management commission could be low or non-existent. A number of external factors impacts the success of one's management efforts; make sure to take this into consideration as you evaluate your career options ahead.

Ownership

Many recruitment firms offer equity, shares, stocks, options, or other types of ownership rewards in the form of a long-term incentive (LTI) to retain internal staff.

If you join at the right time and progress your career enough to be eligible for these rewards to vest, this could become a powerful additional income stream. The theory here is that if the firm ever takes money from a private equity partner, gets acquired, or merges with another firm, the possession and accumulation of LTIs could balloon into a big payout.

There are people who have earned anywhere from 6-7 figures in LTI payouts, but keep in mind, this isn't guaranteed. More importantly, it is certainly not the norm!

There are many strings attached to equity programs and they are the most substantial in earlier stages when the company is being built up. Some are complicated and will only be rewarded to you if certain seniority levels, tenure, or billing targets are reached.

In general, the younger the firm, the bigger the equity opportunity. For more mature firms, because the shares are being divided across a bigger population, each individual share and payout probability is diluted.

At the same time, there is no guarantee that young recruitment firms will actualize the growth they aspire to hit. Thus, LTI incentives are usually a hit or miss. Again, read the fine print and think carefully about the legitimacy of what's being offered.

> ⓘ *As attractive as this sounds, be very careful. There are many cases where the promise of equity exists but never materializes. Worse yet, executives and managers can change equity programs and qualification targets any time.*
>
> *There also are cases where the equity is awarded but the cashout event never transpires!*
>
> *Overall, do not be bamboozled by recruitment firms who dangle the equity carrot to convince you to accept lower compensation packages in the short term.*
>
> *This is a common tactic by many firms to drive loyalty, retention, and commitment to the firm without necessarily paying market-rate rewards and commission in the short term.*

With all these elements of compensation, agency recruiters earn a combination of concrete and intangible rewards. Ultimately, everything is subject to change and of course, switching agencies will impact what you can earn as well.

Long story short, when it comes to compensation and rewards, recruitment firms never rest on their laurels; they constantly look for new ways to keep their staff happy, motivated, and engaged.

Up next, let's dive into the intricacies of commission structures in Chapter 8 to explore this paramount compensation component that deserves its own detailed rundown.

> **Chapter Highlights:**
>
> - Recruitment firms offer a wide range of compensation components, including all expenses paid incentive trips, bonuses, luxury goods, travel experiences, base salary/draw, commission/base salary increases, LTIs, and common corporate benefits such as healthcare, PTO, and 401k plans.
>
> - Recruitment firms are creative in creating compelling compensation components that aim to drive producers' desire to bill more money for the firm and will oftentimes create short-term and long-term incentives to retain and motivate staff.
>
> - No two recruitment firms have the exact same compensation component mix and commission model, a complicated topic that warrants its own chapter, coming up next.

CHAPTER 8

COMMISSION

In both direct hire and staffing business models, the revenue generated from each placement is significant.

However, it's critical to remember–recruiters who are working for a recruitment agency are not pocketing the entire fee for themselves. Instead, they earn commissions off of the profits they generate for the recruitment firm they work for.

Every firm offers different setups, percentages, and rules around what portion of each deal is commissionable.

In most commission models, the producer will only commission off of *their* portion of the deal.

For example, if a 180° recruiter found a candidate to fill someone else's job, they will earn credit for a certain percentage of the deal value, determined by internal guidelines governing shared deals.

Every firm assigns different percentages of the deal, apportioned to different people depending on their role and how many people are involved.

Instead of having to split the deal 2 or 3 ways, full-desk producers can commission off of 100% of their billings, which is only fair as they procured the client, managed the account, *and* placed the candidate.

With that being said, split-desk sales and recruitment professionals benefit from scalability. Thanks to the division of labor, collaboration, and economies of scale they can achieve together, they may earn just as much, if not more than full-desk recruiters, despite having to split deals to commission off of.

Thus, it's incredibly important to understand how each firm is set up without assuming anything. Depending on what the commission rules are, the eventual income earned could be drastically different.

Keep this in mind as we go through the various commission models for both direct hire and staffing professionals in this chapter.

Direct Hire Commission Models

In the USA, the two most popular commission models specifically for direct hire recruitment professionals revolve around a base or something called a draw.

Similar to Goldilocks and the Three Bears, there are 3 main commission structures with increasing risk but also increasing rewards.

Low Risk/Low Reward Model: High Base Salary Plus Low Bonus

Some recruitment firms pay their staff a high guaranteed base salary with a small portion rewarded in the form of discretionary bonuses totalling anywhere from 15-30% of the base.

This is a common compensation structure executive search firms use to pay their junior staff. Many executive search firms use this model because they need people to execute on administrative and support tasks versus optimizing for performance. They need a legion of stable staff to support a couple rainmakers at the top who take home the bulk of the rewards.

While the salary in this model may be higher than average for a junior recruiter at a rate of $65k-$85k, due to the bonus being discretionary and relatively low of a percentage, overall earning potential is limited.

A drawback to this model could be that it doesn't encourage junior recruiters to push to become top performers or grow their skill sets quickly because there is very minimal financial benefit and incentive to do so.

This compensation model is most attractive to risk-averse individuals who aren't in a rush to aggressively upskill which is why they're okay with earning less overall and the slow pace of responsibility advancement.

Other than exec search firms and some boutiques, most recruitment firms are not that interested in compensating people like this because recruitment firms want to generate more revenue per head.

More importantly, recruitment firms want their staff to be self-motivated! They want to hire ambitious people who are driven to do more than just support searches.

Therefore, the next two commission models are more common for the *majority* of direct hire recruitment firms.

Medium Risk/Medium Reward Model: Low Base Salary Plus Commission

Next up is the base salary plus commission model which is commonly offered at midsize and large recruitment firms, especially UK agencies.

By paying a base salary that is lower than in the previous model, firms can hire more staff due to overall lower average cost per head resulting from the savings on base salary spend.

The low base provided is guaranteed so it also helps the employee get situated, offset some of their fixed costs like rent, and pay for some expenses while working hard to bill and earn commissions.

The base is *intentionally* designed to be slightly lower than what's comfortable to incentivize production instead of allowing complacency to set in.

Furthermore, recruitment typically takes some time to understand, coupled with long deal cycles on direct hire (usually ranging from 1 month to 6 months for the recruiter to be paid commission). Thus, recruitment firms who hire large groups of junior staff have to hedge their bets and pay lower bases to account for all these factors.

The reality is that a high percentage of entry-level hires will not end up succeeding due to the difficulty and grueling nature of this job at the outset. Many people lose hope that they'll ever commission, struggle to survive on the low base, and therefore quit the business.

The number isn't formally tracked for the industry, but most agencies have about 60-70% turnover of junior recruiters (anyone who has been in the industry for less than 18 months). Our industry is notorious for fast failure rates; no large recruitment business is immune from such a high dropout rate.

Many rapidly-scaling firms hire entry-level recruiters at $40k-$55k in most major metropolitan cities. In cities like NYC with a high cost of living and regulations on overtime, the base salaries are on the upper end of the range as employers have to adhere to new regulations and changes in state laws on wages as it relates to non-exempt versus exempt employees.

In lower cost of living cities and cities without such stipulations, the salaries can be as low as $35k-$40k which is why this profession tends to attract junior talent straight out of college when they can afford such a drastically low base!

While some recruiters have taken such low salaries, that's not the norm especially with inflation rearing its ugly head in recent years. Salaries have steadily crept up to maintain pace with employment law and account for cost of living increases.

> ① *While $30k-$55k sounds like a very low base salary, compared with most sales jobs, it is a decent salary that is more than adequate to get true go-getters situated as they'll quickly work hard to exceed their base salary by earning commissions.*
>
> *With commissions, it's possible to break 6-figures (or come close to it) within the first year of recruitment for most top billers.*
>
> *Additionally, since all legitimate recruitment firms hire their staff on a W-2 basis, they provide benefits like healthcare, PTO, inhouse training, 401k plans, etc. which is <u>not</u> the case for many other sales careers.*
>
> *Compared to traditional W-2 jobs, recruitment may seem low-paying, but compared to most other sales jobs, the setup recruitment firms provide is generous from the get-go.*
>
> *To put things in perspective, salespeople in real estate (realtors) have a $0 base, receive $0 healthcare benefits, have to pay for their own hardware and software tools, and are liable to learn on their own dime, pay for their own credentialing and courses to pass tests in order to get licenses to practice.*
>
> *Sellers of financial wealth products and insurance similarly receive extremely low base salaries as entry-level recruits. If they fail their financial tests to get licensed, they're liable for those costs, and will not even be allowed to work!*

Due to the very real possibility that most people who try out recruitment don't end up staying, companies intentionally keep base salaries low for entry-level hires to have them prove themselves before raising their compensation bands as they progress through their billing targets.

As promising as many aspiring salespeople project themselves to be, recruitment companies staunchly adhere to low base salary ranges to hedge against the high failure rate of new recruits.

Agencies over-index on finding individuals who willingly bet on themselves to earn the majority of their income through future commissions. They specifically target confident and ambitious people who don't mind an initial low base salary as they're reasonably confident they'll succeed at sales and earn commissions quickly.

In this model, commissions are usually paid out either monthly or quarterly, on top of the base salary. Each recruitment firm has different commission timelines and payment schedules so be sure to read the fine print.

More important than *when* commission gets paid is *how much* you'll be eligible to receive from each deal.

Many firms that offer a base + commission plan pay commission according to a tiered structure, where you're eligible to receive a higher percentage of commission for each additional tier reached. The purpose of this type of structure is to incentivize recruiters to bill as much as possible to reach the highest commission tier.

The tiers are typically determined by starters (candidates who accept a role and start their new job) for the commission period (typically monthly or quarterly).

To illustrate this, let's say you're on a monthly commission schedule consisting of the following tiers:

Tier	Billings (Monthly)	Tier Percentage
1	$0 - $20,000	10%
2	$20,001 - $40,000	15%
3	$40,001 - $80,000	20%
4	$80,001+	25%

If you bill $85,000 in placement fees, you'll have to calculate each tier separately and then sum up all the numbers to arrive at the total commission you'd receive, like so:

Tier 1 total = $20,000 × 10% = $2,000.00

Tier 2 total = ($40,000 − $20,001) × 15% = $2,999.85

Tier 3 total = ($80,000 − $40,001) × 20% = $7,999.80

Tier 3 total = ($85,000 − $80,001) × 25% = $1,249.75

Total Commission Earned = $14,249.40

Keep in mind: In a tiered structure, *do not* multiply the *entire* $85,000 by the highest percentage. *Unless explicitly stated otherwise*, tier percentages do not, by default, retroactively apply to previous billing tiers.

Similarly, a quarterly commission schedule could look like this:

Tier	Billings (Quarterly)	Tier Percentage
1	$0 - $60,000	10%
2	$60,001 - $120,000	15%
3	$120,001 - $240,000	20%
4	$240,001+	25%

If you hit $60,000 in billings for the quarter, you'll earn $60,000 × 10% = $6,000 in quarterly commissions.

If you hit $255,000 in quarterly billings, calculate every tier and then sum it all up, like so:

Tier 1 total = $60,000 × 10% = $6,000

Tier 2 total = ($120,000 - $60,001) × 15% = $8,999.85

Tier 3 total = ($240,000 - $120,001) × 20% = $23,999.80

Tier 4 total = ($255,000 - $240,001) × 25% = $3,749.75

Total Quarterly Commission Earned = $42,749.40

This is a perfect illustration of how lucrative this business can be! Commission checks can rival many people's annual W-2 salaries which is the main reason why this profession is so attractive!

Comparing the two commission schedules above, you can see that the quarterly commission schedule actually could benefit the producer a lot more because it's easier to hit the higher tiers if you give the producer more *time* to rack up deals.

Mathematically, it's difficult to achieve massive value consistently every month in order to hit the top level commission tier because a month is too short.

Monthly commission structures indirectly encourage producers to push all their starters into the same timeframe to max out commission bands in a practice insiders call "sandbagging". This isn't ideal because it could cause recruiters to manipulate start dates to serve their own financial agenda instead of what's best for the candidate and client, leading to increased risk and potential friction.

In a quarterly commission schedule, while recruiters have 3 months to max out the commission tiers, they must also wait 3 months to get their commission payouts! Thus, agency recruiters must always ensure that they can survive on the base salary and manage their spending diligently.

Some firms may create "super" biller bonuses which are paid out once an abnormally high level of billings is reached. All of these additional structures are designed to reward top performers more than average producers for the revenue they bring in.

In this base salary + commission model, recruiters are typically paid out based on the candidate's start date, *regardless of whether or not the client has paid the invoice.*

Always be sure to double check *exactly* how the commissions are calculated, under what conditions they're paid, and what timeframe they're paid. Don't be afraid to ask clarifying questions so that you can fully understand your commission structure and what to expect.

The top billers in this structure have the potential to earn good money. However, as they continue to bill higher amounts, their net* commission rate might decrease based on the percentages offered in each tier. Mathematically, breaking down and summing up the commission values from each tier can result in lower earnings compared to billing the entire amount at a higher commission percentage.

*Net Commission Rate = (Commission + Base salary) ÷ Total Billings

Thus, while this plan is certainly more aggressive than a marginally higher flat rate base with low bonuses, it may not be lucrative enough for top billers over time.

This is why firms in recent years have improved their commission structures in order to pay top billers more so that they will be less likely to leave.

Even so, many companies that offer base + commission structures end up paying net 30-40% commission rates which is not enough for experienced top billers who aspire to earn more.

For those who want the highest rewards possible, the draw model may be more attractive.

High Risk/High Reward: The Draw Model

In the USA, a popular commission model that *many* direct hire recruitment firms offer is called the "draw" or working off of a "draw" because the producer is "drawing" their monthly salary from their future commissions.

A draw functions like a base salary and is paid out on a bi-weekly schedule like a regular paycheck. Annual draw values range from $40k-$65k at most recruitment firms.

Even though the monthly draw feels like a salary, it technically isn't.

As you start producing revenue, the commissions you earn will be paid out to you but *only upon* you covering your draw.

Until then, you're just "drawing" upon your future commission earnings.

Well, why is this possibly a good deal considering you're now getting essentially $0 as a base salary since you're borrowing against your future commission?

The key reason is that draw models offer the most competitive and aggressive commission percentages.

Under the draw structure, both the employer and the employee split the risk of startup costs by not relying on a base salary and electing to "draw" from their future earnings.

Unlike the base + commission structure which pays on a monthly or quarterly schedule, draw models typically utilize YEARLY tiers.

A yearly commission schedule could look like this:

Tier	Billings (Yearly)	Tier Percentage
1	$0 - $200,000	45%
2	$200,001 - $400,000	50%
3	$400,001 - $600,000	55%
4	$600,001+	60%

The draw commission percentages quoted in this chart are common. If the draw commission percentage in the starting tier is lower than 30%, that could be a cause for concern. The percentages have to be high (at least 40%) in order to justify working off of a draw.

Recruitment firms have operating and overhead costs so they can't deviate too far from the numbers provided which is why starting tiers range from 40%-50% with top tiers rarely, if ever, exceeding 60%-70%.

If the recruiter bills $200,000 a year on this commission plan, they'll earn 45% × $200,000 = $90,000.

If the recruiter bills $450,000 a year, they'll earn the following tiers:

Tier 1 total = $200,000 × 45% = $90,000.00

Tier 2 total = ($400,000 − $200,001) × 50% = $99,999.50

Tier 3 total = ($450,000 − $400,001) × 55% = $27,499.45

Total Yearly Earnings = $217,498.95

Net Commission Rate = $217,498.95 ÷ $450,000 = 48%

The math works out so that whether the draw is $50k or $100k, the total W-2 income would stay the same because commission payouts are calculated on a percentage basis off of total billings, inclusive, NOT on top of, the draw value.

On a lower draw amount, you'd commission faster. Conversely, high draws are hard to beat because it will take longer to accumulate enough billings to cover the draw. This is why most recruiters want a draw that's somewhere in the middle, not too high and not too low.

Of course, because they are borrowing against future commissions, there is more pressure inherently involved. If they aren't closing deals consistently, the amount owed on their draw can accumulate month after month, which is stressful.

Although the wins can certainly be huge (net commission rates are much higher in the draw model), the months leading up to covering the draw could feel demotivating.

For junior billers who blanked (billed nothing) for a few months, their draw could feel impossible to overcome due to how many months have passed since they closed a deal. They may lose hope that they'll *ever* beat their draw.

In the draw model, agencies follow the "paid when paid" rule: the invoice must be paid *first* before paying commission out to the producer.

Because the agency is paying such a high percentage of the invoice amount out in commission, they need to make sure the recruiter is also helping out on ensuring that the invoices are paid before receiving their cut. This is also a way to minimize any potential fraud in the rare cases where people try to pad their billings or act like a deal went through when it didn't.

Thus, while draws pay out a much higher net commission percentage, it may take longer to receive the actual payout due to having to wait for clients to pay first.

This is why having the inside scoop on commission plan variety is so critical. Now, you're armed with the information to decide what works best for you to suit your appetite for risk!

The easiest way to think about how direct hire recruitment firms design their reward structures is to notice this pattern:

The more risk you take *upfront* as a biller, the more you'll be rewarded on the backend. The less risk you take *upfront*, the lower your backend rewards will be.

As you progress in this business, small changes in commission rates and structures may have a big impact on your net pay. Do the math in order to make sure you're getting fairly compensated for your billing achievements and contribution to the firm.

Commission Thresholds

In some cases, a recruitment firm will offer a higher than average base salary but build a backdoor clause to reclaim their higher initial investment, called a "commission threshold".

If the minimum amount of billing, the "threshold", is not reached by a certain time, the producer is not eligible to earn a cent of commission.

In this model, because the producer has opted for a higher upfront yearly base, they're sacrificing commission income potential on the backend.

For example, a recruitment firm could offer a $75,000 base salary with a $60,000 quarterly threshold.

While the base salary sounds attractive for an entry level recruiter, this could actually be a terrible commission plan!

The math works out that if you bill $60,000 every quarter, you'll have only met your threshold, not exceed it. Thus, you won't receive a cent of commission despite billing $240,000 for the year at that same rate of production!

This would mean a net commission rate of $75,000 ÷ $240,000 = 31%, a much lower payout than what's possible in other commission plans.

Prohibitively high thresholds may deter and demotivate many potential top billers to continue their agency recruitment career because they won't see any money outside of their base salary.

This further contributes to the existing high attrition rate for our industry. Worse yet, this plan allows billers to optimize and coast on higher base salaries rather than motivating themselves to earn commissions on the backend.

Because many entry-level recruiters were not armed with the inside knowledge shared in AR101, they were unaware of the potential negative impact of a high threshold on their earning potential, naively consenting to such stipulations.

As an insider, it's my duty to warn you–plans with high commission thresholds unquestionably merit a closer look!

Staffing Commission Models

The earning potential for staffing professionals is substantial, driven by the consistent and compounding nature of contractor revenue.

Staffing professionals earn commission off of every hour their consultants work which makes contract staffing commissions a *residual* income stream that is reliable and scalable.

Direct hire lacks this element. In direct hire, once the candidate is placed and the fee is paid, there are no more residual payouts*.

*Other than in extremely rare cases where contracts are negotiated to bill on future earnings past year 1 as discussed in Chapter 5.

Although the percentage amount earned per contractor per week usually isn't nearly as high as you'd commission off of perm deals, you may actually earn more over time as your book of contractors increase, leading to a compounding effect on your income.

The base + commission model is industry standard for staffing professionals so total income is calculated as follows:

There are very rare cases in which companies would offer a draw for staffing professionals. This would be completely out of the ordinary, however some boutiques may propose this model in order to offset their risk. It's certainly not the norm. Most experienced staffing professionals would not go for it because they are paid very well, negating the need to take such a risk.

Compensation of Staffing Professionals

*Commission is calculated per a defined structure as part of the employment contract, varies per firm.

Due to contractors on- and off-boarding week to week, commissions are usually calculated by multiplying weekly spread by the commission rates that are listed on a commission schedule with various billing tiers. Similar to direct hire, you would have to sum up commission values for each tier to get the total commission value for that week.

Commission Calculation

*Commission rate follows clear tiers and guidelines

Keep in mind, the weekly spread is a total of all of your spreads across each contractor that you have out billing for you that week. The numbers per placement may all differ because you'll have different client bill rates, candidate pay rates, and hours per week worked.

> ⓘ As detailed in Chapter 6, while most staffing firms operate on a split desk, with salespeople and delivery specialists working together to fill reqs, some firms (primarily those from the UK) have staffing professionals work on a full desk.
>
> In a split desk model, in order to calculate commission earned, the producer first needs to determine how much of the spread they contributed to.
>
> In other words, split-desk producers cannot commission off of the full spread since they need to split the deal with their colleagues, usually half-half with their internal counterpart.
>
> On the other hand, full-desk staffing professionals, since they did the whole deal, would commission off of the whole spread. Make sure to keep split v full-desk in mind as you go about calculating income potential and commissions.

Similar to direct hire commission plans, commission tiers payouts for staffing professionals increase at higher levels of billing to incentivize producers to make more placements.

A tiered staffing commission structure could look like the following:

Commission Structure

Weekly Spread	%
$0 - $6,000	5%
$6,001 - $10,000	8%
$10,001 - $20,000	11%
$20,001 - $30,000	15%
$30,001+	20%

Staffing commission structures function similarly to direct hire with each tier paid out at its respective rate by default, unless explicitly stated otherwise.

According to this schedule, assuming each tier is paid at its corresponding rate, if you achieve a weekly spread of $6,000, maintained for an entire year (which equates to 52 weeks), you would earn $6,000 × 5% × 52 weeks in commission which equals $15,600 a year.

If you're on a $60,000 base, your yearly compensation would be $15,600 + $60,000 = $75,600 total compensation.

If your weekly spread grows to $15,000 a week maintained for an entire year, you would earn the following amounts:

Tier 1 total = $6,000 × 5% = $300.00

Tier 2 total = ($10,000 – $6,001) × 8% = $319.92

Tier 3 total = ($15,000 – $10,001) × 11% = $549.89

Total Weekly Commission = $300.00 + $319.92 + 549.89 = $1,169.81

Total Yearly Commission = $1,169.81 × 52 = $60,830.12

Total Yearly Earnings = $60,830.12 + $60,000 = $120,830.12

If you're a super biller and you hit $35,000 in weekly spread, maintained for an entire year, you would earn the following:

Tier 1 total = $6,000 × 5% = $300.00

Tier 2 total = ($10,000 – $6,001) × 8% = $319.92

Tier 3 total = ($20,000 – $10,001) × 11% = $1,099.89

Tier 4 total = ($30,000 – $20,001) × 15% = $1,499.85

Tier 5 total = ($35,000 – $30,001) × 20% = $999.80

Total Weekly Commission = $4,219.46

Total Yearly Commissions = $4,219.46 × 52 = $219,411.92

Total Yearly Earnings = $219,411.92 + $60,000 = $279,411.92

> ⓘ *For simplicity, we're utilizing a constant weekly spread number, however in real life, the weekly spread is constantly shifting as some contractors get onboarded while others are offboarding.*
>
> *Also, some contractors don't work a full week while others work overtime, so these numbers are rarely static.*
>
> *Similar to direct hire, never assume these commission plans are without thresholds. Sometimes, if a staffing professional has a very high base, there could likely be a minimum weekly spread number to be hit before a single cent of commission is paid out. These factors could greatly influence earning potential.*

As shocking as these numbers are, especially on the higher end of billing, you must understand how long it takes to get up to these billing numbers. Success does not materialize overnight.

To increase weekly spreads, you would need a substantial amount of contractors working for you which takes time to accumulate as people are constantly starting and finishing projects, all at different times.

Another important element to note regarding the pay of staffing professionals is this: the base salaries of someone billing $6k, $15k, or $35k weekly could be very different!

Since staffing professionals are paid a base salary, they receive promotions, which manifest into base salary increases. As they grow past certain billing milestones, their base salary rises. This is to retain top performers and reward them for billing more and more.

Someone billing $35,000 weekly spread is likely also earning more on their base salary compared to a $10,000 weekly spread biller, leading to even higher all-in compensation for top staffing producers.

Split desk staffing sales professionals are even more valuable because they can bring substantial revenue to their employers. Since each project or contract could be worth multiple 6-7 figures over time, top staffing salespeople could be huge gamechangers for their employers. Because of the high revenue potential they can generate, they're paid more than direct hire full-desk producers, earning as much as $80k-$150k on base salary alone.

Staffing is an incredible way to build wealth, and it's not abnormal at all for top recruiters and sales leaders to break $150k-$300k in total earnings per year as early as 2-5 years into the business. Some even achieve $500k-$1mil in W-2 income per year within 5-8 years of their career.

While the money is great, nothing comes for free!

The reason why staffing professionals are paid so much is that they have to remain connected, engaged, and supportive of their clients and contractors at all times. In some markets, contractors work odd hours or do overnight shift work and the staffing professional is expected to be available should any issues arise.

The stress of constantly having to oversee contractors to ensure their performance is satisfactory, painstakingly monitoring client/candidate progress and feedback, or something as simple as making sure contractors properly update their timesheets, can be grueling and stressful.

The revenue per placement is wonderful and the profits are residual, but you have to keep an eye on everything. This type of pressure is troublesome and exhausting, unlike direct hire where as long as your candidate passes the guarantee, the transaction is done with no further hassle.

This tradeoff of effort and stress undoubtedly is reflected in the income potential difference between direct hire and staffing.

On the bright side, staffing professionals are locked into a solid base which helps them solely focus on building up their business without covering a draw and they can benefit from an exciting commission proposition with plenty of room to grow.

For both direct hire and staffing professionals, commission numbers and compensation plans are never static.

Based on market conditions and firms' operational structures, agencies may adjust their commission and compensation structures at any time, leading to both positive and negative ramifications on producers' income opportunity.

Of course, if changes to commission plans end up hurting you more than you're willing to accept, it may be time to evaluate new agencies to work for. Producers are free to switch agencies as they see fit, but commission plans rarely remain static over time.

Therefore, it's important to understand commission schedules, tiers, and conditions as you start and build your career to make sure you're getting rewarded in a fair and incentivizing way.

Chapter Highlights:

- Direct hire recruitment firms offer either a base salary or a draw.

- The commission potential for mid to top performers on a draw has the potential to be more lucrative than a base salary plus bonus/commission structure.

- Commission thresholds may impact total earning opportunity so take this into consideration when evaluating commission plans.

- Staffing professionals are paid on a base salary and earn commission off of every hour worked by their contractors according to a tiered commission schedule.

- Weekly spread therefore weekly commissions rarely remain static as contractors are often on- and off-boarded.

- The combined value of high markups and recurring temp revenue allows staffing firms to profit immensely off of establishing strong client relationships, candidate networks, and specializing within high margin niche markets where they can build market share.

- Staffing professionals can offer direct hire more easily than direct hire professionals can offer staffing because staffing is more complicated while direct hire is easier to understand and execute on.

CHAPTER 9

THE AGENCY RECRUITMENT CAREER LADDER

Agency recruitment is a unique profession that has its own career ladder and progression pathways.

This chapter is an overview of common career trajectories agency recruiters can choose to undertake.

Keep in mind, agency recruitment is a choose-your-own-adventure career! There are twists and turns that could happen, so there is no "right" way to grow within this business.

That being said, here are common roles with increasing responsibilities you'll encounter in the agency recruitment career ladder, starting with sourcer.

Agency Recruitment Career Ladder

Owner or Exec
Director/Manager
Sales/Full Desk
Recruiter
Sourcer

Sourcers & Researchers

Some recruitment firms may choose to employ staff to help with the most junior task, sourcing candidates for roles and researching market data to help senior team members.

Sourcing may entail sorting through high volumes of information on platforms such as LinkedIn and job boards to build out lists of candidates relevant to searches, in a process called "market mapping". They can also be responsible for carrying out different projects for clients like putting together compensation reports or other data for clients and candidates who want analyses on their market and competitive landscape.

Some researchers and sourcers may be responsible for finding candidates' contact information and tasked with reaching out to candidates for initial conversations. Some fulfill a more administrative and internally-facing role, so they may not be involved in customer engagement of any sort. Depending on where the sourcer works, their job remit could look very different as duties vary firm to firm.

In many executive search firms, entry-level staff are hired mainly to assist their more seasoned colleagues on recruitment, search, and research projects. These are the folks most commonly paid out on a base plus minimal bonus structure.

In recent years, many companies have outsourced this function to countries and regions such as India, the Philippines, and Latin America due to the simplicity of this role, resourcers' lack of client-facing duties, and low costs to hire.

Recruiters

Recruiters primarily responsible for full-cycle split-desk recruitment are the next step up in the career progression ladder.

This role includes sourcing duties along with calling, referral-networking, job-board prospecting, and LinkedIn messaging promising candidates in order to have them interview for open reqs or pipeline them for future representation.

Recruiters may be expected to manage the entire recruitment process or can pass off the candidate to their sales counterpart who then takes over the interview management and deal closing process.

As with all roles depending on where you work, there are variances in terms of expected skills and responsibilities. More or less, recruiters are mainly tasked with candidate-side duties.

As recruiters grow in their career, they can progress in 3 ways:

1. They can learn the sales side and move into a full-desk recruiter/headhunter role.

2. They can transition fully into sales and become a split-desk client-facing professional.

3. They can stay exclusively on the split-desk recruiting side, either becoming a senior recruiter (individual contributor) or a recruitment manager, then director, overseeing a team of split-desk recruiters.

As previously stated, every agency recruiter has different wants and needs so while some recruiters may want to progress into sales, others may never take interest in making the pivot.

Sales and Full-Desk

As recruiters continue to progress their career, naturally, they'll inevitably be faced with the choice to enter and grow on the sales side of the business.

Split-desk staffing sales professionals and full-desk direct hire agency recruiters both engage in sales activities such as: cold-calling clients, wining and dining clients, organizing entertainment and events, putting together and/or attending speaking opportunities and conferences, and arranging/leading special panels sponsored by the recruitment firm.

In direct hire, it's especially critical for headhunters to really understand the search and have a relationship with both parties—client and candidate—to build the relationship smoothly through the whole process.

As deals start closing, full-desk headhunters switch from poaching and building relationships with candidates to chasing down new business leads in order to pipeline and land new reqs.

Top performing sales-side staffing and full-desk direct hire professionals are always in high demand as sales prowess is commercially more valuable than recruitment skills which are easier to train producers on. Selling requires ingenuity and fearlessness to cold call tough clients, which most people find intimidating and hard, thus top salespeople are prized as critical team members within all types and sizes of recruitment firms.

In order for salespeople to succeed, the recruitment agency will usually cover all client activities and reimburse salespeople fully for the costs of all of these events, including paying for transportation, conference tickets, client entertainment, meals, and lodging to win new and repeat business.

Every firm has their own reimbursement policy so make sure to clarify each firm's client/candidate entertainment strategy and reimbursement policy before incurring any of these costs.

While the hope is to generate business as soon as possible, patience is required to track and follow the clients and candidates through their recruitment needs. Top salespeople strive to build exclusive relationships so when the time is right, they have a competitive advantage and benefit from being first on the scene.

In order to further boost conversion rates and increase brand awareness, many agencies have invested in building a social media presence and marketing as well. This is still an area of growth and development that many salespeople are trying to integrate into their existing outreach strategies and market approach.

Director/Manager

Oftentimes, a highly successful recruiter or sales leader is identified as a role model and top performer internally, so they're usually first in line to be considered for career advancement.

Official titles for these promotions could be Managing Director, Division Director, Branch Manager, Manager, Team Manager (associate - senior level), Senior Manager, Associate Vice President, Vice President, Managing Partner, Partner, etc.

Every firm creates their own titles, qualifying activities to progress, and career levels, so the same title could mean different things to people working at different agencies.

Regardless of their title, this role consists of working with their immediate team to set and achieve billing targets, problem solve, train best practices on sales and recruitment, drive company-wide initiatives, run monthly reviews, provide daily workflow support, and work through mental health and other personal struggles.

What's more, they're responsible for internal recruitment both for their team as well as others. They help evaluate resumes, interview potential hires, market the company brand, and work with senior leaders to decide who to hire and promote.

Some people at this level elect to continue billing, thus being more of a billing manager as a player-coach. Others who don't want to bill anymore progress into a non-billing manager position.

If people at the management level continue to produce on their own desk, they'll still earn their due commissions while also earning a team override, a bonus that is derived from their team's production, covered in Chapter 7.

For team members who fail to reach their revenue targets, they must be managed on a strict performance plan until they get back on track.

① *Unlike other careers where management is expected and recommended as the natural next step to progress, agency recruitment does not necessarily follow this conventional advice and career path due to how individual contributors (ICs) and managers are compensated.*

In traditional careers, management promotions lead to significantly higher base salaries and career status which is not always the case in recruitment since many top billers earn more as an IC due to the power of commission income, reducing their financial interest to walk away from production.

Managers, ironically, may end up earning less than top billing ICs due to how low overrides are should their teams underperform and losing their own commission income by stepping away from billing.

Since individual production is paid out at a higher percentage where one is in control of their time and abilities, arguably staying an IC can pay top billers a lot more than taking a risk to manage a team who ultimately fails to bill.

Even if they do bill, overrides are paid out at such a low percentage compared to personal billings that it could lead managers to earn less!

Certainly not helping the issue, managers only receive a small base salary increase (if any) to manage since recruitment firms by nature are stingy on base salaries, preferring to reward more on commission. Thus, the small base salary increase for managers largely falls short, woefully inadequate to compensate for the time and effort it takes to get juniors up and running.

Uniquely in agency recruitment, choosing to become a manager may actually decrease income potential due to the high failure rates of entry-level hires combined with the immense quantity of labor hours and effort required to properly develop staff.

Furthermore, top billers are treated well and constantly praised for their outsized contributions to the firm. They enjoy all the attention they receive, the high income they earn, and their role as a biller. Managers, instead of being the star, would have to train future stars, a responsibility top billing ICs may not enjoy.

There are instances where management makes strong career sense for recruiters and sales leaders.

Whether they aren't motivated by commission anymore, are sick of being client/candidate-facing, or simply want to try management to see what it's like, moving into a management role may be the right next step to achieve their career objective.

Owner of a Recruitment Firm

Many top billers who have succeeded at an agency for quite some time may find that they're ready to break off on their own to run their own recruitment business.

This is ultimately the apex of the agency recruitment career–owning a recruitment firm.

As top billers build their sales and recruitment experience, they gain more confidence in their capabilities to produce so they may, at some point, become ready and willing to pursue self-employment. Instead of splitting commissions with their employer, they prefer to work for themselves.

Over time, top billers who have wisely managed their money may accumulate enough wealth to comfortably quit their job. This makes entrepreneurship tenable while greatly reducing their risk of failure.

However, while "owning a recruitment firm" may sound prestigious and advantageous, it's not necessarily the right move for the majority of top producers.

> ⓘ Running a business is challenging, stressful, and not without risk.
>
> Due to how lucrative and entrepreneurial this career is, many agency recruiters build an incredible and fulfilling lifestyle and business for themselves and for their employer. To leave all that behind isn't a decision to make lightly!
>
> Plus, the recruitment firm pays for all tools and resources, support staff, annual salaries, commissions, health insurance, and all other operating costs, simplifying the producer's life and workflow.
>
> They can earn a lot of money doing less since their employer handles all back office and back-end duties. Unlike recruitment owners who must worry about covering all financial obligations and executing on operational tasks, producers need only to focus on what they do best: selling and filling reqs.
>
> Especially for high earners such as staffing sales leaders, leaving their employer could be financially devastating because they'll lose all the support from the recruitment, back office, and finance teams that help them maintain and grow their contractor volume. To replicate a similar sized book of business would require an immense investment of capital, time, and effort, thus many sales leaders prefer to stay with their existing firm.
>
> As mentioned earlier in Chapter 7, since recruitment firms are built, sold, and/or invested in by private equity/venture capital firms often, being an employee with an ownership stake at a successful agency could still be lucrative while providing more work-life balance with much less headache.
>
> Lastly, many small recruitment businesses stay small, often ending up with one person running the show as a solopreneur and/or may struggle to retain and attract staff past a small team. Some top billers miss the camaraderie, resources, and stable growth opportunity they have working at bigger firms providing more support to top billers.

There are many reasons why many top billers *can* run their own recruitment firm, but *choose* not to. As with everything in recruitment, careful thought goes into selecting what is the right setup for you to align with your unique personal and professional needs.

Other Roles within Recruitment Agencies

As much as some agency recruiters thrive and enjoy this career as a lifelong profession, some want to try something new.

Here are some examples of other roles within recruitment agencies available:

Internal Recruitment

As recruiting firms grow, they also need internal recruitment staff!

Internal recruiters for recruitment firms usually have previously worked at an agency and gained a deep understanding of the role, therefore they're capable of credibly explaining the job, pay structure, lifestyle, and expectations to potential new recruits.

They work with senior leaders within their firm to advertise and promote the business and career opportunity to entry-level hires and also opportunistically poach top billers and seasoned talent from their competitors. They recruit for all other roles the recruitment agency needs as well, such as office administrators, HR people, trainers, and back office support staff.

Learning and Development (L&D)

Larger agencies who train classes of entry-level recruiters typically employ a L&D (learning and development) team, consisting of former agency recruiters and/or sales trainers from other realms.

They're expected to build curriculums, create resources, design worksheets and training materials, coach staff at all levels, and work with senior teams to understand their team needs.

The courses and training modules they're tasked with creating and delivering include topics such as recruitment, sales, client management, management and leadership best practices, communication, how to motivate teams, and business strategy.

Marketing

Since this industry is so niche, marketing specialists who have a background in recruitment may have an edge over marketing generalists to promote recruitment services to target customers.

Marketing specialists working at recruitment firms create ads, videos, interviews, articles, and graphics to be showcased on a variety of mediums including social media to help the company promote their brand and services.

Marketing teams also support internal hiring efforts, document and promote fun company events, shout out promotions, spotlight top billers' success stories, and share exciting company information with the public.

Recruitment companies who have developed a strong marketing presence benefit massively through the positive publicity they generate which helps to attract new hires at a faster rate and win market share for the firm.

This is a function with immense potential to grow in the future with more recruitment agencies recognizing the increasing value and necessity of AI-assisted marketing efforts, social media, and other promotional tools.

Administrative, Financial, Legal, and Business Operations for Recruitment Firms

Like all businesses, recruitment firms need administrative, financial, legal, and operations staff which include back-office, accounts payable/accounts receivable teams, as well as contractor management and compliance help.

These functions help with the invoicing process, daily oversight of contractors out on billing, legal review of recruitment contracts and dispute resolution, accounting, payroll, and other critical business functions.

Some senior leaders can afford support staff in which case they'll also hire office administrators and/or executive assistants.

Since agency recruiters already have a strong understanding of the inner workings of their firm, leadership, and clients/candidates, these are all functions that they can pivot into.

As much as this career ladder covers some traditional career paths and alternate career routes available to agency recruiters, no one recruiter will have the same exact mindset, time frame, and career progression experience, nor are they required to.

You can take your career in whichever direction you choose. Once you've done this job, you'll have gained useful skills that will help you succeed in any endeavor, whatever it may be!

> **Chapter Highlights:**
>
> - Recruitment careers start from the most junior level (sourcing and research) up to running your own agency.
>
> - People can do anything and everything within the career ladder as no recruitment career is considered "standard", rather following personal preference and strengths.
>
> - Top billers often are faced with the option to set up their own recruitment firm but may decide not to do so. This is completely up to each individual to decide by weighing the pros and cons based on their own professional and personal preferences.
>
> - Recruitment firms also employ other types of professionals in roles such as internal recruiters, L&D trainers, support staff (legal, backoffice, accounting, contractor management), and executive assistants.
>
> - The variety and breadth of experience people gain from this career helps them transition into other disciplines and career paths smoothly and successfully.

CHAPTER 10

TRAITS OF TOP BILLERS

Based on my experience in the field and my current role as a headhunter for top billers, I've observed that while everyone is unique, many top billers exhibit similar traits.

The majority of top billers tend to display all or most of these 9 common traits:

1. Strong Financial Drive

In this challenging sales career with low base salaries, commissions are the name of the game! In order to succeed, one must have the desire to produce revenue and generate income, thus topping the list is possessing a strong financial drive.

As much as we'd like to think people organically and altruistically just want to do good work, to succeed in this competitive market, good is often not good enough to "make it" in this business.

Too often, people underestimate the *continuous* hard work required to become a top biller and instead lose steam halfway through their careers.

Without desire for exceptional monetary reward and success, why go the extra mile to earn commissions?

Most wouldn't! Those who undertake the Herculean effort to build a successful recruitment practice are few and far between.

Everyone's "why" is different but the result is the same: it pushes top billers to do what average producers *won't*. Motivation and drive to succeed cannot be manufactured artificially by outside pressure; it has to come from within.

Thus, the "why" behind a producer's financial motivation is the most important element, the core driver to do the hard things required to persevere in this profession.

Those who are sincerely money motivated will not settle for less. They will work the extra hour and go the extra distance to earn the extra dollar.

Even after reaching success, top billers continue to strive for more as their financial ambition is ingrained in their identity. To realize their financial aspirations, top billers adopt a "no excuses" mentality, which segues nicely into the next trait.

2. Accountability

Since recruitment is an entrepreneurial job predicated on a desire to achieve, a high degree of accountability is required in order to be an effective professional.

This isn't like other job functions where you can skate by and hide among the inefficiencies of a large team. Since this career fixates on *personal* production, very few exceptions can be made if billing goals aren't achieved within a timely manner.

Regardless of whether you're self-employed or work for someone else, you're responsible for *everything* as this job is very demanding on you to manage every element of the placement process.

Therefore, agency recruiters have to treat their career as their own business and take full ownership of it, with all outcomes resulting from their efforts or lack thereof.

Top billers have a can-do and will-do-at-all-costs attitude, largely self-imposed, because they feel a deep sense of personal pride to be the best they can be, to do the best they can do. To become a top producer, they rely on the next trait.

3. Confidence

In order to go from zero to hero, possessing a deep sense of confidence is quite possibly the biggest ingredient top billers rely on.

Because so many entry-level agency recruiters enter the industry after a few years or right out of college, they're young in age, experience, and exposure to the professional world. In previous roles, they may not have liaised enough with senior leaders and executives, clients who they're now tasked to interact with.

Furthermore, the vast majority of people getting into recruiting do not start out as experts in the field they recruit for! This additionally makes them feel like an imposter when first speaking to candidates and clients, most of whom are much older and subject matter experts (SMEs).

To overcome this hurdle, it's crucial to conquer self-doubt and worry, while simultaneously cultivating a profound sense of self-worth, a resolute commitment to success, and unwavering confidence.

Entry-level recruiters can leverage their energy, personality, availability, and coaching skills to more than make up for their lack of knowledge and experience in the technical market!

Top billers believe that their intellect, ability to learn, and people skills supersede all else, thus they're unafraid to engage with executives and leaders on equal footing.

More importantly, they spend their time on a more difficult task: communicating their value proposition effectively to draw business and patrons to them despite competing against more seasoned competitors–one of many skills top billers possess.

Remember, a headhunter's job revolves around understanding market dynamics, recruitment life cycles, understanding what's important to the stakeholders in your market, distilling key information, and being a great coach and cheerleader your customers can rely on.

Interestingly enough, it's not the depth of technical knowledge that predicts a recruiter's success. Heck, even years of experience don't matter that much in this business as many talented recruiters in their first 1-2 years have outbilled others with decades of experience!

Instead, it's the recruiters *themselves* that can change their production outcome with the right adjustment in approach, work ethic, and strategy. This is because clients and candidates gravitate towards people who are likable and possess a positive, can-do demeanor. Those who display an aura of confidence come off as reassuring and trustworthy regardless of their level of technical knowledge.

This could happen within a shockingly short period of time because when you put your mind to something, believe in yourself, *and* do it properly, anything is possible.

All in all, top performers do not shy away from touting their skills and capabilities, reflecting their strong self-belief, thus winning others' respect (and business!) as well.

4. Perseverance

In order for any headhunter to establish solid footing, they have to be patient, perseverant, and tenacious to make a lasting impression on their market to stand out. Sometimes, it may take weeks, months, and years(!) to extract top talent and crack key accounts.

Recruitment is a tough job that requires consistent effort which keeps recruitment fees high! Even though a lot of people are initially attracted to the possibility of making a lot of money in recruitment, many fall off the bandwagon early on as they discover how hard building a successful recruitment practice actually is.

This is also a tough job because people are unpredictable. You can't control how your clients and candidates may behave towards you or to each other. Not only will you have to obstinately fight your way through any issue, you have to always remain one step ahead by playing chess while others play checkers.

In sales careers like recruitment, hardly anything is smooth sailing. Clients and candidates get mad. They lose their cool. They're unreasonable at times and will lash out. They can mess things up and blow their chances, which kills your deal prospects, causing stress, anxiety, and disappointment.

Through thick and thin, top billers forge ahead, even in the face of constant disasters, roadblocks, and setbacks. Their unyielding optimism and exceptional problem-solving skills shine no matter how much pressure they're under.

5. Mental Stability

Being that recruitment is a type of sales job and sales jobs are notorious for being hard to succeed at, mental stability is something that warrants serious discussion for anyone considering this role.

In this profession, it's up to the individual to maintain a calm outlook and stable composure to handle the rollercoaster of emotions you're bound to face in this business.

Since this job is reliant on other people and their decision making processes, you can execute your role perfectly, but others may not. Thus, anything and everything can go awry. Not only that, you may be personally blamed and misunderstood by both external and internal stakeholders for anything that goes wrong.

To make things worse, conflict and negative experiences are guaranteed to pop up. We're dealing with people and people a*lways* come with drama. It's never predictable as to when something or a series of things will blow up in your face.

This uncertainty further compounds because agency recruiters have to satisfy external stakeholders and hit revenue targets. Other careers are internally-facing and unrelated to profit generation so this is less of a problem. However, for sales careers like recruitment, this type of pressure could be all-consuming and lead to "burn out" if not managed well.

For all these reasons, agency recruiters have to find ways to maintain their mental wellbeing in order to perform at their best.

In order to execute at the highest level, compartmentalization is a key skill to exercise consistently. In this profession, managing emotions and developing self-discipline are critical skills.

What you say and do matters greatly so you have to be on your A-game when engaging with clients, prospects, and candidates. Since reputation is everything in this business, an off day or having a few bad conversations could lead to severe consequences due to how fast word of mouth news travels.

People who don't have the mental and emotional maturity to deal with problems in a healthy and productive manner struggle to grow professionally in this particular line of work.

The reality is that if you want to make a LOT of money, you will have to deal with a LOT of drama and stress. This is why tough jobs like agency recruitment pay so much!

That being said, anyone can succeed in this career—with practice, training, dedication, and prioritization of personal development.

6. Effective Communication Skills

Like in all sales jobs, superb communication skills (reading, writing, and speaking) are a must-have trait for top billers.

Clients will judge you on how you sound on the phone, from your behavior in person, and how well-written your email prospecting is.

This is why communication is everything in this profession! You only have a few seconds to catch a prospect's attention; how you communicate makes all the difference.

While some top billers come into agency recruitment with exceptional reading, writing, and speaking skills, others learn it and perfect it on the job. In either case, top billers never stop dedicating time and effort to improve their ability to communicate and connect with others.

7. Emotional Intelligence (EQ)

In order to win clients and candidates, top billers leverage their deep understanding of human psychology and behavior to create rapport and build genuine relationships which is why possessing high EQ (emotional intelligence) is a foundational trait for success in sales careers.

If people like you, trust you, and enjoy speaking to you, they'll naturally choose to partner with you over others.

> ① *The best resource to improve your EQ is How to Win Friends and Influence People by Dale Carnegie. The importance of business and personal etiquette is paramount to winning the hearts and minds of your customers.*

Becoming an agency recruiter is a great way to develop your EQ. By watching, observing, and mirroring the behaviors of others, you can increase your emotional range and understanding of different personality types.

Whether in person or through the phone, be sensitive to ensure prospects feel heard and catered to. Err on the side of caution, think carefully before you speak, and give your prospects your full attention.

The small details, polite gestures, please's, and thank you's strengthen your relationships and elevate your status in the eyes of your prospects because they feel that you care.

Don't ever forget, we are in the people business so they always come first. Without *people*, there is no *business*.

While top billers may vary in their approaches and styles, they always ensure that their customers feel valued and supported.

8. Desire to Win

In any sales job, a top priority interviewers look for is a track record of competitiveness. However, I like to call this trait "desire to win" because results are the only thing that matters in this business.

Results-orientation geared towards a mindset of winning is what keeps someone dedicated to their work at hand with a longer term vision. The point isn't to just "try your best to *compete*". The point is to "try your best to *win*".

While being competitive certainly is a strong drive, it also may lead to toxic behaviors against your customers where you'll want to argue or put your ego above the deal which can ultimately hurt your reputation in the market and stop the deal from progressing.

A mentality to win requires strategy, intellectual thought, foresight, and patience; it goes beyond competing for the sake of being competitive, sometimes a bit aimless of an endeavor and an ego pursuit above all else.

In other words, the goal is to win the war (desire to win), not the small battles (competitiveness). Winning frivolously and arbitrarily due to one's competitiveness could lead to adverse consequences.

Top billers are often diplomatic, generous, and big-hearted because they understand that letting clients and candidates win in the short term is all part of the game. Giving others an *illusion* of power and control ironically leads to eventually gaining the strategic upper hand.

Inevitably, those with a deep desire to win often have more staying power to achieve than those with superficial motivations that flame out quickly.

This desire to win isn't a nefarious, winner-takes-all, zero sum game. In fact, it is quite the opposite. Wanting to win should extend into a collaborative win-win mindset to help all parties reach a mutually beneficial outcome, making the role more fulfilling!

Work as a united team, not as adversaries to your clients and candidates. Advance their agenda and advocate on their behalf to consistently win.

Plus, it is more fun to view cold-calling, marketing, and prospecting with a gamification mindset than feeling a sense of pressure or fear. With a desire to win, you can turn something intimidating into something exciting and stimulating.

To this day, I still love figuring people out and winning them over; it brings me joy to make others happy.

9. Eagerness to Learn

In today's economic environment, the speed of technological change is so intense that if you don't adapt quickly, you may fall behind. To remain competitive, even the most talented and savvy recruitment professionals *have to* find interest in learning and evolving.

A good example of some changes lately have been centered around the advent of social media marketing and proliferation of personal branding on sites such as LinkedIn.

Plenty of old-school recruiters lose market share simply because they don't have the marketing wherewithal to make it through the noise. The internet, social media, and AI are powerful tools that are slowly changing the game more and more with each passing year.

Part of the change is natural monopolization by the companies that already are leveraging today's tech and marketing options to promote themselves better than their competition.

Another new development is the pay-to-play model; some companies simply are spending more on marketing through sponsored ads, which helps them attract customers.

Whether utilizing free or paid marketing strategies, the companies who are more visible consistently win market share.

It may sound frustrating and unfair, but the truth of the matter is that quality isn't the core driver of who wins. This will always hold true in any industry: the most well-marketed individuals and businesses will continue to consolidate market share.

To combat this issue, keep updated on modern ways of communicating with your prospects (social media content marketing) while continuing to leverage best practices of yore (cold-calling, meet & greets, setting up client events).

Both modern and past strategies have to be leveraged. Running a business evolves every year. As things change, top billers are smart and humble enough to learn new skills and experiment with innovative products and resources, adjusting their strategy accordingly.

It's not a matter of personal preference; it's what you need to do to survive and thrive that counts, so having a learner's mindset helps to keep current with new and improved business practices.

Note on Introversion vs Extroversion

As you probably noticed by now, I purposefully have not mentioned introversion or extroversion as a trait. It's because there is a BIG misconception and bias that salespeople need to be extroverts, which I vehemently disagree with.

Some of the BEST people in this industry *are introverts or fall somewhere in the middle as ambiverts*!*

*An ambivert, according to Oxford Languages, is a person whose personality has a balance of extrovert and introvert features.

This may be surprising, but because so much of this job is about empathizing with customers, introverts and ambiverts may actually have a competitive advantage.

Uber aggressive, in-your-face, rabidly extroverted salespeople actually fare poorly in recruitment! They have a tendency of talking over customers or selling too early which actually turns candidates and clients off.

This personality type, while useful in selling widgets or used cars, falls flat in selling high-end recruitment services to executives and senior candidates. This specific customer demographic doesn't respond well to mass-market sales techniques; rather, it demands a touch of sophistication and refined business etiquette.

To survive and thrive in this tough sales job, you have to be able to listen to people and work through their issues. Contrary to popular belief associated with the sales persona caricature, introverts thrive especially well in this particular type of sales job since it's more about written, verbal, and listening skills rather than who has the loudest mouth and brashiest demeanor.

In fact, silence is such a powerful skill during sensitive salary negotiations that again, introverts, who tend to be much more calm, collected, analytical, and strategic, have a distinct advantage.

That being said however, whether or not you are a natural extrovert, introvert, or ambivert, you can succeed at recruitment! You just need to be highly attuned to your strengths and weaknesses as it relates to your natural communication style and effectiveness at work, so self awareness is key.

If you're an extrovert, you can benefit from forcing yourself to speak less, ask more questions, and intently listen to prospects instead of rushing into the selling process.

If you're an introvert, when the time comes to share your input and aggressively sell to push the deal through, you must have the fortitude to communicate forcefully as well.

Whatever the case may be, you must be versatile and switch between communication styles, tones, and strategies. Stay vigilant and monitor your own behavior to overcome any challenge that comes your way!

Hopefully, this chapter can serve as a helpful self-assessment resource and benchmark as you continue to explore how this profession could align with your natural strengths.

Chapter Highlights:

- Like in all industries, there are certain characteristics and traits that predict success in each field. The 9 traits top agency recruiters exhibit consist of: strong financial drive, accountability, confidence, perseverance, mental stability, effective communication skills, emotional intelligence, a desire to win, and eagerness to learn.

- Contrary to popular belief, the odds of success in recruitment does not correlate with level of extroversion. In fact, highly extroverted people who are too aggressive and unable to listen to their customers usually do terribly in recruitment. If they are to stay in this industry, they will need to work hard to mitigate this weakness.

- Some salespeople may succeed more in other sales careers but struggle in recruitment because this business is all about emotional connection, placing more importance on listening and relationship-building skills rather than pushy sales tactics.

Questions to Consider:

- Think long and hard about your financial WHY's here. What are the WHY's driving your desire for financial success?

- What are you looking to achieve from this career?

- Why do you think recruitment uniquely could be a good fit for you and your skills?

- How many of these qualities do you possess? What are some examples (this will help with interview prep)?

- How does this career potentially align with your lifestyle, goals, and personality?

CHAPTER 11

RECRUITMENT TOOLS

In order to keep organized, agency recruitment professionals utilize a number of different tools to run their business smoothly.

Here are some tools recruitment firms utilize:

Customer Relationship Management Tool (CRM)

Since agency recruiters work with high volumes of people everyday, the best way to keep organized is to use some sort of Customer Relationship Management tool, commonly referred to as a CRM.

Most recruitment agencies buy a subscription to a CRM system for each member of their team. Alternatively, some choose to use a free CRM software. Some agencies even create their own proprietary CRM software.

Due to the volume of people interactions every recruiter has, it would be impossible to remember everything which is why a good CRM tool is a critical function recruiters can't live without!

By inputting all the notes and details from conversations and digital communications into the CRM, you can log and access key information about candidates and clients and know exactly where to pick things back up from.

Furthermore, if you're working at a large recruitment firm, the CRM also allows internal team members to view each other's candidate and client activities to minimize crossover and duplication.

Most recruitment teams set strict customer contact rules (usually timebound) to limit recruiters prospecting the same contacts. A CRM helps everyone adhere to internal policies, record recent activity, and work together seamlessly.

A proper CRM also provides a search function for you to easily compile lists of the right people to reach out to using the tagging and categorization features, making compiling customer lists easier and faster.

Lastly, the CRM doubly functions as a KPI tracker and report generator to help internal teams and senior management keep tabs on their staff's daily and monthly activities.

Applicant Tracking System (ATS)

Every recruitment firm has used their clients' Applicant Tracking Systems (ATS) and/or uses their own.

These systems allow candidates to directly submit their applications, track candidates in process, notate what stage the candidate is at, record when interviews are happening and at what stages, and log metrics about reqs and candidate volume.

As CRMs become more powerful tools absorbing many ATS functions, recruitment agencies can pull in candidate information received from applicants who've applied to the recruitment agency's roles.

Clients may also want agency partners to log candidates into *their* ATS portals in order to track submissions and minimize duplication due to potential "candidate ownership" issues.

"Candidate ownership" refers to the right to submit and represent a candidate who has not applied to the client directly or been represented by another recruitment firm within a set time period per contract terms (usually 1 year from the date of candidate profile submission).

If a candidate has already applied directly to a client's ATS or was submitted by another recruitment firm within the negotiated time frame, that would disqualify the candidate from being re-submitted. The ATS system would flag the submission as unacceptable so the recruiter won't be able to represent them.

The ATS system helps clients protect themselves from agencies who try to earn an additional fee off of a previously submitted candidate or a candidate who self-applied.

Similar to a CRM, since ATS programs capture candidate and interview data, that information can be helpful for recruitment agencies to figure out which metrics translate into deals, helping them figure out which KPIs are important and how high to set them.

Job Boards

Job boards are still a big component of advertising for recruitment firms. Despite the low amounts of viable candidates coming through job boards, they still yield some promising candidates from time to time.

Recruitment agencies can buy advertising slots on third party, industry-relevant job boards that are specific to the markets they serve. They also can utilize their own website's job board to showcase their impressive portfolio of reqs available in hopes of attracting strong applicants.

Job boards are still worth utilizing because candidates still use them! If you can place a candidate you find off a job board, the profits generated from that placement will more than cover the cost of utilizing and advertising on the platform.

Every agency has their preferred set of job board subscriptions, either fee-based or free, on which to advertise their open reqs to potential candidates. One of the biggest players is LinkedIn, which deserves its own section as it's such a vital platform so many agency recruiters use.

LinkedIn

LinkedIn is a powerful professional social media networking site that agency recruiters fervently use to access market data, advertise, self-promote, and reach out to client and candidate pools.

Since professionals want to stay in touch with their colleagues, build their professional credibility and track record, and access potential employers, LinkedIn profiles are constantly updated to reflect real time changes.

LinkedIn has become the go-to tool for this express purpose, which differentiates it from all other social media platforms, providing them a near-monopoly when it comes to professional networking.

One of LinkedIn's most powerful functions is the ability to access entire company organizational structures. Due to users' self-reporting, LinkedIn can help agency recruiters build out org charts and create market maps that are highly accurate and current.

Few professionals, especially in white-collar roles, *don't* have a Linkedin presence! It's *the* platform that not only showcases the most up-to-date information on prospects, but also allows recruiters to message and send connection requests to them!

You can also pay for more features such as posting job adverts, sponsoring ads, and accessing specialty programs like LinkedIn Recruiter and Sales Navigator which are widely used by recruitment firms with ATS/CRM integration potential.

Often, employees at LinkedIn work with agencies to find more bespoke solutions and access even more data. LinkedIn itself is incentivized to work with recruitment firms, a big portion of their customer base (and revenues)!

Most importantly, LinkedIn allows you to create massive amounts of free and paid content across a variety of options: video, written (posts and articles), as well as graphics (ads and posts with pictures).

You don't even have to pay high advertising fees to enjoy the benefits of using LinkedIn! As of this writing, due to the high cost of LinkedIn ads, unsponsored content still has a very large reach for a couple of reasons.

Your first degree connections' network can see the content that they engage with so it gets pushed out to a broader audience. Furthermore, LinkedIn welcomes producers of content to create a massive amount and variety of information to populate and disseminate on their feeds.

Since so many clients and candidates use LinkedIn, this tool provides a win-win situation for both the platform and agency recruiters: agencies pay LinkedIn for access and tools, and LinkedIn helps agency recruiters identify, connect with, and curate relationships with candidates and maximize branding opportunities.

As mentioned, for most career verticals, LinkedIn is the holy grail that has everything you could possibly need to find and access candidates and clients. It is a critical tool, a lifeline, a core platform most recruiters can't live without.

Social Media & Other Platforms

In addition to LinkedIn, there are no limits to what platforms recruitment agencies can leverage.

Some agencies and agency recruiters curate a strong presence on Instagram, Facebook, Twitter/X, Tiktok, YouTube, and will continue building branding efforts on any new social media platform that becomes mainstream in the future.

Due to extremely low levels of regulation, agency recruiters can freely promote, market, and design whatever they'd like on social media with little limitation on what can or cannot be said.

A number of social media ideas recruitment firms can create content on include: job search advice, tips on how to work with recruiters, open reqs the recruiting firm currently has, interviews with key people in their specific industry focus, etc.

Additionally, many recruitment agencies have even ventured into the podcast space along with video content across multiple platforms in order to promote their expertise and business brand.

Some agencies have even created their own apps to make life easier for their subscribers and users to apply to jobs and get notifications about their candidacy.

Overall, this space of social media marketing for recruitment agencies continues to be an ever-evolving, diverse, and wide-reaching sector that is still in early stages with plenty of room to grow.

As of this writing, social media content is viewed as optional by the industry, but as these platforms and consumer behaviors evolve, it will become a must-have definitive edge in order to gain a competitive advantage in the coming decade.

A Note on Artificial Intelligence (AI)

Recruitment is on the cusp of another revolution - the advent and rapid ascension of AI capabilities and tools.

When LinkedIn first emerged, the same fears existed - many people predicted the end of recruitment because they surmised LinkedIn would automatically connect candidates and clients together, cutting headhunters and staffing firms out.

However, the exact opposite happened!

Because LinkedIn was pervasive and easily accessible by everyone, it very quickly became congested, noisy, and hard to navigate! Only the most perseverant, creative, charismatic, and brave headhunters were able to penetrate their markets to build and win market share.

Ironically, LinkedIn enabled recruitment firms' profits to grow and accelerate due to the information on the platform being so transparent and how cleverly top billers utilized this tool.

Candidates and hiring managers were finally aggregated transparently into one single platform, thus they became easier to identify and contact. Thus, instead of LinkedIn taking away market share or replacing recruiters, recruiters leveraged information found on LinkedIn to build their business!

My prediction is that the EXACT same will happen with AI. Creative and committed individuals will utilize these tools in their favor, not to their detriment.

AI can help reduce labor hours wasted in two major areas: content creation and outreach efforts. Simple tasks that are administrative can slowly be outsourced to AI instead of having to hire someone locally or abroad to do it. This is an exciting advent bound to benefit many recruitment firms and recruiters. Again, new technology tools have the capability to help recruiters make more money, not less!

Of course, the adoption speed and pervasiveness of these tools will vary drastically as everyone has different needs and levels of willingness to invest in deploying new tools and strategies.

While AI can absolutely help with many elements of a recruiter's daily tasks, it cannot run itself without direction and human oversight.

Computers cannot replace actual humans because of the high-touch nature of recruitment, especially when it comes to cold-calling, building rapport, curating true connections, offer negotiation, troubleshooting, and conflict resolution. This is for certain and stands the test of time.

Payrolling System

Every recruitment firm has their own system they use to manage their internal staff's payroll as well as the contractors they've placed.

Direct hire recruitment firms are overall much cheaper to operate due to not having any costs associated with payrolling contractors.

Of course, staffing firms have to find other ways to manage this costly hurdle. Some outsource to a third party agency that specifically works with staffing firms to manage payroll needs for their contractors. Some employ support staff internally to carry out this function. Every firm has different setups and costs when it comes to payrolling.

Direct hire recruitment firms similarly utilize a variety of systems, platforms, and software/support vendors, but operational costs are relatively and comparatively low, especially those with a small staff, solopreneurs, or mom and pop recruitment firms.

Regardless of firm type and size, most companies focus on their business of billing and driving business as a priority and outsource their tech needs.

If anything, vendors servicing recruitment firms have proliferated, reducing costs further! The oversaturation of software products, many of which are provided by overseas developers, ensures that recruitment agencies will keep benefiting from decreasing software costs coupled with an expanding array of product options.

Every firm has their own preference of what systems to utilize, functionality required, and price points they're comfortable paying per user. There isn't a fixed approach or a single prescribed tech stack (a combination of software programs) that agencies use.

Be sure to inquire about the tools and resources available to gain a better understanding of how each recruitment business is structured to assist you.

Chapter Highlights:

- Recruitment firms use a number of vendors, platforms, and recruitment software to help their businesses run smoothly, most or all of which are outsourced to vendors who specifically target and service the recruitment sector.

- Recruitment firms need a CRM and ATS system to manage candidate and client engagement, and record all interactions, KPIs, and other data they need.

- Recruitment firms also use LinkedIn and other social media marketing platforms for outreach and building brand awareness to win more market share.

- AI will enhance existing tools and create new products recruitment professionals can utilize to grow their business. It's not to be feared but to be embraced and leveraged.

- That said, rest assured, recruitment still needs the human touch as candidates and clients certainly don't convince themselves of what they need to do without the direction, support, and influence of top recruitment professionals.

Recommended Next Steps:

- If you need help crafting your social media strategy, check out our Social Media Marketing for Agency Recruiters Course which covers this topic in depth with actionable steps at dgrecruit.com/courses.

CHAPTER 12

LAUNCH YOUR CAREER!

Agency recruitment isn't your typical career; everyone has a different journey into how they "fell into" this industry.

Here are various ways people have launched their career in agency recruitment:

Referral

A decent contingent of agency recruiters find their way into the industry by being directly referred into the role by someone they know who works at a recruitment agency.

Since so many large and midsize recruitment firms hire college grads or early career professionals, many young people who get into the business naturally spread the word with their networks.

Plus, they're influenced by their employers to do so, eligible to earn referral bonuses should they succeed at attracting new hires to join the firm.

As firms are constantly growing due to attrition, employers often ask their staff to prospect any salesy friends they may know that could be interested in this career.

Thus, a straightforward way to get into this line of work is to go through your contacts and connections on LinkedIn and see if you know someone who can refer you into the business.

Because of the power of word of mouth marketing and high degree of trust for candidates who are referred, this is one of the most common ways you can launch your recruitment career.

Success is contagious and good people usually know other good people, so referrals are a reliable source of future recruitment talent.

Campus Recruiting

Recruitment firms often partner with colleges and other institutions to exhibit during job fairs to attract talent. Internal recruiters and top billers at recruitment firms are tapped to represent the company at these recruitment fairs to prospect, interview, and attract more candidates for the firm.

Many successful recruitment professionals will often be sent to their alma mater to lend further credibility as a great case study highlighting this career's potential. Like many other industries, new grads are a great source of affordable, hard-working, and unencumbered candidates who can prioritize working due to their life circumstances.

Not to mention, new grads are easy to train as they have no bad habits or limiting mindsets as it relates to recruitment and sales, so they can be molded from the very beginning.

Some recruitment firms also offer internship opportunities which could be an invaluable experience as you get to try out the job firsthand ahead of graduating. Thus, keep an eye out for recruitment firms hiring at your campuses offering both full time roles and internships.

Apply to Recruitment Agencies Directly

Many agency recruiters get into this career by applying directly to recruitment firms that are hiring internally or for one of the firm's clients.

By leveraging the knowledge you've gained from AR101, the DG Recruit Podcast, my YouTube videos featuring top billers' journeys, and the Recruiter Prep course, you now possess a deeper understanding of this business and career than many professionals already in the field!

Make sure to share the information you've learned about the career as you go about researching and connecting with recruitment firms and leaders in your local area. Apply directly to recruitment firms' job ads with clear indication of wanting to become an agency recruiter. This is a straightforward way to successfully launch your career.

In addition to submitting your applications, proactively reach out to senior recruiters, managers, and directors using LinkedIn and email prospecting. Send them a simple message to highlight your interest in recruitment, what you know about it, why you think you'd be a great fit, and ask to connect more on the phone to discuss the role further, etc.

Since success in recruitment is dependent on leveraging sales skills throughout the interview process, recruitment firm owners and employers *especially* appreciate a good prospecting note!

Feel free to make yourself known by reaching out to them directly, aggressively, and purposefully. This shows that you're committed to the industry, understand the profession's intricacies, and can execute on your goals.

Be fearless to tenaciously reach out to any and all recruitment firm contacts in the location or setup that may work for you. Through your efforts, hopefully you'll be perceived as a promising and attractive hire.

3rd Party Introduction

Once people decide they want to pursue a career in sales and recruitment, they may also consider joining a junior sales/recruiting bootcamp or seek out R2Rs like DG Recruit.

While most of my business is concentrated on placing experienced top billers, there are a few clients who would consider entry-level hires and pay us for this service.

However, hiring is usually limited to considering candidates based in major metropolitan cities like NYC, Austin, Miami, and other high growth areas. Being that most entry-level recruitment jobs require staff to be in the office 4-5 days a week, potential candidates must live within daily commuting distance of these hot spots.

If you are interested to check if DG Recruit could represent you as a candidate, please contact us at dgrecruit.com.

Furthermore, a few recruiting firms have intentionally partnered with sales boot camps or recruitment courses (such as ours, recruiterprep.com) in order to prospect course graduates to join their firm.

While this is a small portion of how recruiters launch their career, the knowledge they gain from working with a R2R or going through a training program helps them get ahead because they naturally have more support and guidance through the course materials to successfully land a recruitment job.

Networking

Since recruitment is such a non-traditional career path, I've even heard of stories where a recruitment owner or senior leader bumps into a random person off the street, strikes up a conversation, and ends up hiring them as an entry-level recruiter. This could be at a store, restaurant, sporting event, social event, or any other venue.

Commonly, the recruitment professional who meets this person will usually try to recruit them to join their team. If the prospect is interested, then one of two things can happen: either the agency invites them in for an interview or nothing comes out of it but the prospect now knows about this career of recruitment.

Sometimes a chance meeting can lead to the start of a new career but most future recruiters network using LinkedIn or attend in-person networking events to expand their circle of contacts. Keep an eye out for recruiters you meet at these events or through your personal and professional contacts.

Some people can find a recruitment job on their first try, while others who are more selective about their preferences or live in locations where job opportunities are scarce may need to expend significantly more effort to secure a role that aligns with their needs.

Regardless of how high or low, fast or slow response rates are, continue your outreach efforts until you see success. This is a great test of your resilience and gives you an idea of what our job entails!

Recruitment firms are always looking for locally-based, highly motivated, and sales-oriented hires so as long as you can present yourself well, you'll increase your odds of launching your career, sooner rather than later.

Chapter Highlights:

- There is no one way to launch your recruitment career as people often accidentally discover this career through a referral, chance meeting with someone who is in the field, or applying through a job board.

- LinkedIn and email reach outs are commonly where you'll gain the most traction with interacting with and establishing first contact with recruitment firms and leaders within those organizations.

- Prepare your pitch to explain why you're seeking to launch your recruitment career and illustrate why you'd be a good fit for the career.

Recommended Resources:

- Take the Recruiter Prep Course at recruiterprep.com to launch your career. Pay special attention to Module 3 which will teach you how to nail your narrative during recruitment interviews.

- Make sure to use the language you discovered in AR101 during your conversations with other recruiters. Learn more about others' experiences and recommendations on how to best succeed within the profession.

- Contact us at dgrecruit.com to request the resume template specifically designed for agency recruiters that I have personally used for all my candidates that greatly helped them lay out their experience efficiently.

CHAPTER 13

NEXT STEPS AND TIPS FOR SUCCESS

Now that you've reached the last chapter of AR101, you know a LOT about this industry, career, and business, not only more than the average person, but potentially more than actual agency recruiters *themselves*!

With everything you've learned from this ultimate insider's guide, you're equipped to launch your recruitment career with confidence.

Beyond AR101, here are more resources you can leverage on your journey:

Complete Recruiter Prep

The first step is to take our Recruiter Prep course at recruiterprep.com for more video and audio coaching to master recruitment interviews and launch your career.

Module 1 is a recap of many of the topics we covered here, mainly what recruitment is all about.

Module 2 helps you distinguish if recruitment is the right career fit for you in further detail.

Module 3 is where the heavy lifting occurs–I teach you how to design your resume, prepare your interview spiel on "tell me about yourself", behavioral interviewing tips, and what to expect during the interview process.

One of the most important features of the Recruiter Prep course is presenting multiple interviews with top agency recruiters and recruitment entrepreneurs. Through the video interviews, you can observe how top billers behave, listen to their life stories, and absorb their advice (available for free on recruiterprep.com, the DG Recuit Podcast, and my YouTube Channel).

Tune into the DG Recruit Podcast

The DG Recruit Podcast at dandanzhu.com/podcasts/dgrecruitpodcast is an invaluable resource during this exploration phase while doubling as a staple training resource for recruiters already in the biz.

Not only will you have more insights on this career, you'll also receive my coaching on different elements of the job like business development, candidate management, career strategies, deal troubleshooting, and some life and investment advice.

My stories and coaching on the DG Recruit Podcast are directly from the battlefield, so they share what actually occurs in the real world *on the job*, not the rosy picture of recruiting people *think* it is.

The DG Recruit Podcast shares how-tos, best practices, interviews with top billers, and war stories from both my recruitment career and as a recruitment entrepreneur. Tune into the DG Recruit Podcast on your favorite podcast platform.

Considerations to Make

As you continue to contemplate a future in this profession, I have some considerations to share that would be worth evaluating as you go about launching your career.

Here are 6 considerations worth careful reflection:

1. **Direct Hire or Staffing?**

In Chapters 5 and 6, you learned about direct hire and staffing. Which one is best for you?

Typically, entry-level recruiters will receive an offer to join a recruitment firm with little choice or control over which market they're recruiting for and what type of recruiting they'll end up doing.

The recruitment firm dictates what the new hire will be assigned to do. As long as the firm offers solid training, has a good reputation, and a strong management team and culture, most recruiters would accept the offer and launch their career in short order.

If you know yourself well enough to definitively commit to a specific type of recruitment from the outset, use that as part of your selection criteria when evaluating opportunities and firms.

Communicate your needs and reasoning when speaking to employers to make sure you're on the same page on what role you're seeking.

2. **Interview MULTIPLE Recruitment Firms**

The more recruitment firms you apply to, the more opportunities you'll access. Reach out to high volumes of potential employers to compare what they're offering and learn more about each firm.

During the interview process, don't hesitate to question and confront your concerns with the interviewers. As always, transparent conversations are fair game that most recruitment professionals are comfortable handling.

Especially when it comes to large metropolitan cities in the US, there is an astounding number of recruitment firms hiring incoming recruitment talent. Exploring more than one firm is undoubtedly best practice in order to learn more about various teams, setups, and commission plans in order to pick the best one for you.

3. Large, Midsize, or Boutique?

As for the importance of firm size, should you work at a large, midsize, or boutique recruitment firm?

While large and midsize firms may have more of a churn and burn reputation, they're likely to hire the highest volume of entry-level recruiters, increasing your odds of being hired.

Once you've worked at a big recruitment firm, you'll have learned everything there is to know about this business since the training and internal resources are so strong. There are many mentors to learn from, many opportunities to grow.

That being said, the competition at large and midsize firms is fierce. Factually, there are more people to compete against from a billing perspective. Additionally, KPI culture is more prevalent at larger recruitment businesses who need to monitor activity levels of every hire to make sure they're on track to hit billing targets.

Therefore, it's important to think of how team culture and work environment may impact your stress and performance levels. Some people love intense competition and don't mind being micromanaged, whereas others may not thrive under that setup.

On the other hand, smaller firms and boutiques may be more laid back and collaborative. However, smaller firms tend to have less robust systems, processes, and training resources with a low volume of entry-level hiring. Socially, there could be fewer coworkers at a peer level to turn to.

If you're at a small firm where average billings are low, it will be very hard to learn best practices to become a top biller. At most large firms, there are potentially more big billers to learn from so this is less of an issue.

Keep in mind: just like in all career fields, there are good and bad leaders at most companies, regardless of size.

This is why it is recommended that you interview as many firms as you can, scrutinize managers' track records, and carefully assess company culture.

Ask tons of questions and be fearless to interview your interviewers. As much as they're evaluating you, you're very much evaluating them.

4. UK or American firm?

As mentioned in Chapter 3, the most common employers in the recruitment sector tend to be American or UK firms.

UK firms tend to be more focused on curating an on-site culture where there are many high-performing and tight knit teams. Top billers grow by leaps and bounds due to the hyper-competitive environment cultivated at UK firms which generate incredible billing numbers in record time.

This level of intensity, pressure, and inter-competitiveness, while fun for some, comes with quite a bit of micromanagement which is why younger people tend to do better culturally at UK recruitment firms. They want the structure, enjoy the culture, and can partake in the happy hours, the extensive socializing, and the brash "banter" in the office.

However, for many, especially more mature entrants into recruitment, that culture may be too aggressive, high pressure, and inappropriate, incongruent with their lifestyle and workplace expectations.

American firms (boutiques especially), on the other hand, while unable to beat UK firms' ability to generate so many top billers in such a short time frame, seem relatively more tame and even-keeled in their expectations towards their staff on billing amounts and progression timelines.

At some American firms though, the rah-rah-rah culture is just as severe, the parties just as wild, and the culture just as competitive as some UK firms.

It's really hard to determine which one is better or worse, as it greatly hinges on factors such as the office, team, manager, and local culture involved.

Thus, the jury's out on this one!

You'll have to interview the firms yourself to figure this out more as culture is impossible to really describe, envision, or predict unless you've seen and felt it for yourself.

Only *you* can make the judgment call on whether it's the right environment for you or not.

5. On-site, remote, or hybrid?

Recruitment is still largely an in-office position if you're serious about achieving the maximum level of success, especially when first starting out. This demanding role requires a dedicated investment in apprenticing under top billers and fully immersing yourself in their environment to absorb their teachings.

That's not to say that there aren't great remote companies that are willing to take a chance on entry-level recruiters and train them up, but there's so much to learn that it's best that you work in the office at least 2-3 days a week, if not, all 5 days, to gain momentum and learn the basics.

Most firms that are willing to and excel at training new recruiters often require an on-site schedule of at least 2-5 days because it's easier to teach staff how to do the job without the distraction of remote working. Furthermore, there are political benefits career-wise to building strong internal networks. This is hard to do if the in-person socialization element is missing.

While there are many benefits to working on-site, more and more recruitment companies, especially smaller ones, are increasingly flexible on hiring people on a remote basis. This trend is likely to continue due to agency recruiters only needing a phone, computer, and internet connection to engage with clients and candidates.

If you're aiming for a remote opportunity, it might require a bit more effort to find, but rest assured, such opportunities do exist.

6. Team Culture

Since internal teams work together closely and motivate each other to stay on task and achieve billing targets, if you can find a supportive and enjoyable environment to work in, your chances of thriving are higher. If you can execute and deliver results, then this is a win-win situation for both employ*er* and employ*ee*.

If you like partying and hanging out with colleagues, find an environment that is conducive to that. If you need your private time and don't like the politics of dealing with a lot of internal colleagues, then consider joining a boutique, smaller satellite office, or a startup that is more close knit.

If you like the hustle and bustle of competition and desire to speak freely and often with similarly-minded colleagues, find a place that encourages and embraces people like you.

If you'd rather keep to yourself, want more privacy, and focus on your work, find a place that doesn't expect your undivided time and attention in order to be accepted socially.

Don't worry or focus too much about finding the "perfect" agency to work for; find the right manager, team, and culture that aligns well with you.

Chances are, if you and your immediate manager get along and take a genuine interest in each other, that bodes well for your future success. Hopefully, they and the rest of your colleagues will be motivated to teach you everything they know so that you can become a better recruiter everyday.

As you build up your recruitment career, after a few years at one agency, you can take the skills you've learned wherever you decide to go next.

Top headhunters and staffing leaders are few and far between, which leaves a lot of space for talented and hardworking people to create a name for themselves.

The need for top agency recruiters remains persistently high, therefore, your career opportunities are endless and abundant as long as you continue to develop your skills and billing trajectory.

10 Tips to Maximize Your Career Success

Once you get into your first recruitment role, this is where the rubber meets the road!

Here are 10 tips to maximize your opportunity and set yourself up for success in this career:

1. Attitude Over Aptitude

So much of success in recruitment relies on possessing a can-do, positive, and solutions-oriented attitude. There is no room for blaming others, despairing, feeling entitled to success without putting in the work, or losing steam.

You have to keep your spirits up and effectively self-manage to maintain an infallibly optimistic attitude through good days and bad.

2. Build *Valuable* Social Connections at Work

In every sales environment, per the Pareto Principle, the top 20% of performers drive 80% of the business results—*those* are the people you want to align yourself with.

Not to sound harsh, but you're not going to win at work milling about with the bottom 80% of performers. The turnover in agency recruitment is unforgiving and they probably won't make it too long.

Thus, it's critical that from day one, avoid negative people with problematic attitudes who like to complain. As they say, misery loves company, so you're better off avoiding toxic people at work who are not similarly motivated and committed.

You become who you surround yourself with so invest in relationships with the go-getters at work who are clearly rising stars. In turn, they'll motivate you, show you what's possible, and keep you on your toes to stay on track.

Politically, this is also the smart thing to do as these people tend to move up quickly and be a great source of support and information at work.

3. **Implement the #7777rule**

From my first week at work, I created the #7777rule to jumpstart my recruitment career: work 7am-7pm (any 12 hour window works), 7 days a week, at least 7 times a year.

This doesn't mean you have to work 12 hour days on Saturdays and Sundays for the rest of your life!

Remember, the #7777rule is only about working *some* time on *some* weekends out of the year. To clarify, you don't have to clock in on Saturdays for 12 hours, you just have to make an effort to consistently focus on recruitment for 7 days continuously to keep up your momentum and focus.

For instance, I'd go to lunch and coffee meetings on Sundays as time permitted for my candidates. Or I'd call through job boards and add new lists of hiring managers I found to my CRM for a few hours on Saturdays. Working weekends allowed me to catch up on my KPIs, get a headstart on the following week's activities, and meet more customers opportunistically!

This helped me level up quicker than my peers who chose to work less hours at the start of their career. The headstart I gained from working weekends helped me build my recruitment business faster to top the billing leagues quickly.

It sounds like a tall order but it's genuinely not.

When you're embarking on a serious career that is difficult to do, focus and hard work are critical to success.

The sooner you enact the #7777rule, the faster you rack up your 10,000 hours of deliberate practice to achieve mastery in a specific skill or field. This idea, popularized by Malcolm Gladwell's book, Outliers, points out that most exceptional individuals often spend around 10,000 hours honing their craft before achieving remarkable success. The same concept absolutely applies to top performers in recruitment.

When you're a junior recruiter, you don't have enough knowledge to take shortcuts and "hack" recruitment.

Gain experience through a high volume of work and effort, specifically in the first few months of being hired–your future self will reap the rewards of upskilling quickly.

> ① *If you delay this learning process by working less at the start of your career, you're only holding yourself back from rapid growth, further providing more opportunities for your competition (internally and externally) to outpace you.*
>
> *The easiest way to make a big splash right off the bat is to distinguish yourself among the new group of hires by outworking your immediate peers.*
>
> *Politically, there is also a huge advantage if your upper management sees you working the #7777 rule. You'll immediately gain recognition and be highlighted as a role model for other junior recruits to learn from.*

This is what's so wonderful about the agency recruitment career: even rookies can very quickly outperform experienced billers by adhering to the #7777 rule.

4. Exceed Your KPIs

On a related note, don't just aim to hit your KPIs. Ideally, *exceed* them.

Not only will it benefit your business and earning potential immensely, it will help you earn brownie points! KPIs are tracked by managers and if they see you working hard to not only hit but exceed your KPIs, that shows an impressive level of commitment to the role.

Plus, exceeding KPIs usually translates to exceeding billing targets! After all, higher levels of activity naturally translate into higher odds of generating placements.

This will greatly enhance your image at work and spotlight you as a standout hire, which leads to more recognition and political clout at work.

5. Enrich Your Success Mindset

To reach aspirational billing and career goals, a healthy success mindset is everything. For some people, that's listening to podcasts sharing stories about highly inspirational people. For others, it could be self-help books, conferences, networking events, or surrounding yourself with other success-oriented people.

Try to focus on the "why" behind your desire for achievement. As Zig Ziglar says in his bestseller *Born to Win*, "desire is the catalyst that enables a person with average ability to compete and win against others with more natural talent."

What is the ultimate vision you're striving so hard to actualize? Double down and commit to making the sacrifices you must endure in the short term to reach your desired outcome.

Self-help, self-care, and self-love are the most fundamental elements of wellness. Find a system that works for you in terms of surrounding yourself with positive people, resources, thoughts, and habits that keep you motivated and on task.

6. Dream Big!

Dare to dream big. A popular concept in sales is "if you shoot for the moon, at the very least, you'll land among the stars".

In other words, you have to dream big at the minimum so that you can achieve a solid outcome even if you don't hit your ideal target performance.

Eliminate fears around failing and most certainly, do not stress about burnout. You have no time to worry. Worry is the most unproductive feeling, emotion, and stressor!

Conduct yourself in a mature, serious, and dignified way and your clients and candidates will respect your confidence. Act as if, and the results will undoubtedly follow.

7. ONLY Do Recruitment

There is nothing as important as gaining your sure footing in this business when you first start. This means doubling down on recruitment, and recruitment only.

Since recruitment salaries start off so low, many people get distracted chasing side hustles for quick short-term cash, instead of focusing on generating commissions.

This is a big, big mistake because they miss the big picture:

Assuming you work in an environment with high earning potential, the commissions in recruitment are much more lucrative than what's possible in most other businesses, let alone small-time side hustles.

Without fully focusing on conquering the tough learning curve required to succeed in recruitment, many people fail to launch because they're already splitting their focus, energy, and time investment in multiple directions, becoming a "jack of all trades, master of none".

Instead, the best strategy to succeed in recruitment is to direct all your spare time and energy into becoming a top biller as soon as possible. Prioritize the opportunity that is likely to have the biggest impact on your life and earning trajectory, rather than wasting time chasing chump change on the side.

Go all in! This will lead you to higher billings faster, maximizing your commission opportunity. This upfront investment of time and effort will pay off.

Don't lose sight of the prize–nail recruitment, and you won't *need* any side hustles!

8. Limit Social Media Distractions

Distractions will hurt your capability to garner success in recruitment because it's disruptive and time-consuming. Recruitment requires your full attention so technology and social media indulging could be absolutely detrimental.

I started recruiting during a time where streaming services and social media tools didn't consume people's daily lives like they do today. Currently, tools are so addicting that even serious professionals struggle to avoid the time suck our devices have become.

Frustratingly, I now struggle with managing screen time doing unproductive things, indulging in watching pet videos, show bingeing, and scrolling through funny memes. Instead of achieving my goals, I often fall into the trap of neglecting mission-critical tasks due to being addicted to cheap entertainment.

I'd argue this is possibly the biggest issue facing everyone today, no matter what field they work in!

In order to combat this, find ways to concentrate without distraction. This won't be easy, but it's necessary; put in the hours and focus at work to generate the results you want.

9. Be Financially Diligent

Due to the low base agency recruiters start out at, financial management is *key* in order to give yourself the time to learn the business as you work towards your first commission check.

Don't commit to signing onto an expensive lease, big ticket trips, or other financial commitments that may seriously squeeze you in months that you don't bill. Figure out ways to save money as much as you can in the early days.

You won't be making commission for a while, so don't take on any unnecessary financial burdens. Hold off on any big financial moves until you start to commission steadily.

10. Challenge Yourself

There are always things you can do better! Commit to a mentality of improving everyday at your craft. Force yourself to ask the questions you're scared to ask. No more procrastination or excuses - eat the frog and do the darn thing!

Whether it's health, wealth, life, or work, you will benefit from investing into challenging yourself to never get too comfortable with the status quo.

I hope these 10 tips can serve as a list you can frequently revisit and review as you start building your agency recruitment career. I'm rooting for you!

Closing Note

Once you start your agency recruitment career, a new door opens!

Not only will you increase your sales prowess, at best, this profession could change your life, creating a wealth of new business, career, and financial opportunities.

With the information you've gained from AR101, the ultimate insider's guide to agency recruitment, you now have a head start to tackle this business and career!

I can't wait for you to experience the joys, excitement, and growth this profession is certain to bring you. Join our Facebook Group at facebook.com/groups/agencyrecruitment101 to share your wins, questions, and challenges. I'll be here to support you all the way!

Cheers to your future in agency recruitment!

Chapter Highlights:

- As next steps, take the recruiterprep.com course to launch your career in three straightforward modules.

- To upskill as quickly as possible, listen to the coaching on the DG Recruit Podcast, especially the episodes about sales and candidate control.

- Evaluate the 6 considerations to make as you go about exploring recruitment firms.

- Review the 10 Tips to Maximize Your Career Success as you embark on your career.

Recommended Resources:

- For books to help motivate you as you continue your journey in sales, please check out my recommended booklist at dandanzhu.com/recommendations.

- For more tips about surviving and thriving in your first year in the industry, check out our ebook DGR Tips for First Year Agency Recruiters available at dgrecruit.com/books.

- Follow me on LinkedIn at linkedin.com/in/dandanzhu for daily inspiration and coaching on recruitment topics.

www.ingramcontent.com/pod-product-compliance
Lightning Source LLC
Chambersburg PA
CBHW050634160426
43194CB00010B/1673